"Like so many evangelical doctoral students I will be forever grateful that someone introduced me to the work of Brian Walsh. If you also hunger for the biblical exposition of John Stott combined with a deep commitment to radical Christian hospitality worked out in theologically diverse, scholarly, Christian community I invite you to wrestle with this collection of Brian's writings. Be prepared to let the struggle in community form a deeper Christian imagination in you."

—BETH GREEN, Provost, Tyndale University, Toronto

"According to Walsh, 'knowing this world is, at heart, a matter of love.' A journey through this book slowly reveals the profound meaning harbored within this deceptively simple statement. Walsh here summons us to a faith that responds with redemptive courage in a time wracked by suffering and upheaval. Rooted in the best of the reformational tradition, his hard-won wisdom speaks urgently to our need for healing, justice, and hope."

—RONALD A. KUIPERS, President, The Institute for Christian Studies

"In a world thin on discipleship and starved for prophetic vision, Brian J. Walsh refuses to be satisfied with the church's terminal nostalgia. Rather than longing for a church at the height of its power (tainted as it is by the impulses of empire) Walsh grounds us in God's present, amplifying Holy Spirit's bold and persistent invitation to join Jesus' healing work through the cultivation of faithfulness, bravery, and imagination."
—ANDREW STEPHENS-RENNIE, Director of Missional Renewal, Anglican Diocese of Kootenay

"Brian's latest book is a must-read for everyone concerned with Christian formation in our current moment. *Of Prophets, Priests, and Poets* brings together the best of Brian's writings on education, Christian formation, and empire in an exquisite example of his poetic, prophetic writing style embodying his message. On every page I discovered insights that resonate with my campus ministry (and whole life!) context, and I will weave these insights into every part of the work I do in Christian formation—and into my whole life as a follower of Jesus in community in this upside-down world."
—SARA GERRITSMA DEMOOR, Campus Minister, University of Guelph

Of Prophets, Priests, and Poets

Of Prophets, Priests, and Poets

Christian Formation at the Gates of Hell

BRIAN J. WALSH

CASCADE *Books* • Eugene, Oregon

OF PROPHETS, PRIESTS, AND POETS
Christian Formation at the Gates of Hell

Copyright © 2025 Brian J. Walsh. All rights reserved. Except for brief quotations in critical publications or reviews, no part of this book may be reproduced in any manner without prior written permission from the publisher. Write: Permissions, Wipf and Stock Publishers, 199 W. 8th Ave., Suite 3, Eugene, OR 97401.

Cascade Books
An Imprint of Wipf and Stock Publishers
199 W. 8th Ave., Suite 3
Eugene, OR 97401

www.wipfandstock.com

PAPERBACK ISBN: 979-8-3852-2856-0
HARDCOVER ISBN: 979-8-3852-2857-7
EBOOK ISBN: 979-8-3852-2858-4

Cataloguing-in-Publication data:

Names: Walsh, Brian J., author.

Title: Of prophets, priests, and poets : Christian formation at the gates of hell / Brian J. Walsh.

Description: Eugene, OR: Cascade Books, 2025 | Includes bibliographical references.

Identifiers: ISBN 979-8-3852-2856-0 (paperback) | ISBN 979-8-3852-2857-7 (hardcover) | ISBN 979-8-3852-2858-4 (ebook)

Subjects: LCSH: Christianity—philosophy. | Christianity and culture. | Christianity and politics. | Education—philosophy.

Classification: BR100 W35 2025 (paperback) | BR100 (ebook)

12/12/25

Unless otherwise indicated, Scripture quotations are from the New Revised Standard Version of the Bible, copyright © 1989, by the Division of Christian Education of the National Council of the Churches of Christ in the United States of America.

For James H. Olthuis
Mentor, Friend, Dancer

Contents

Acknowledgments | ix

Introduction: Christian Formation at the Gates of Hell | xiii

1. Of Prophets, Priests, and Poets: Autobiographical Reflections on the Calling of Campus Ministry | 1
2. Transformation: Dynamic Worldview or Repressive Ideology? | 18
3. Thinking "Christianly" Revisited: A Dialogue | 38
4. Education for Homelessness or Homemaking? The Christian College in a Postmodern Culture (*Co-authored with Steven Bouma-Prediger*) | 49
5. Meredith on the Subway: A Story of Displacement and Homemaking | 69
6. Poverty, Justice, and the Fruit of the Spirit | 80
7. Faithfulness and Justice: Reformed Faith in the Face of Empire | 90
8. On Not Forgetting Who You Are: A Targum | 114

Bibliography | 133

Acknowledgments

The vision of education and ministry on offer in this book is rooted in an understanding of human life, knowledge, and formation that is decidedly communal. The modernist idea of the autonomous individual is an abstraction at best and an idolatry at worst. Not only are humans inescapably formed in the context of community, the very interrelatedness of all things in creation bears witness to a communality that goes all the way down. Unsurprisingly, what is true of human life in the communal context of all of creation and the Creator, also happens to be true of all human products, including books.

 I am sure that most readers of this book will concur that their best work, the richest moments in their life, and the places where their lives most flourished, all happened in the context of work shared in community with others. That is certainly the case in my life. It is not for nothing that most of my books over the years have either been co-authored or written in community. Even this book, published under my name, has a co-authored chapter. So, my first indebtedness is to my co-authors: J. Richard Middleton, Steven Bouma-Prediger, Sylvia Keesmaat, and the Wine Before Breakfast community at the University of Toronto from 2001 to 2020. You will all recognize your contribution to my life and my thought in the chapters that follow.

 My partners in campus ministry and scholarship are too numerous to list, but I want to acknowledge that I've done my best work in community with the late Hendrick Hart, N. T. Wright, Andrew Stephens-Rennie, Deb Whalen-Blaize, Dave Krause, Geoff Wichert, and Aileen Verdun. Thank you, friends, plus all the other good partners in ministry over the years. Amanda Jagt was not only a partner in campus ministry, where she demonstrated beautiful skills in the shaping of liturgy, she also applied her literary eye to an attentive edit of these chapters. Thank you, dear friend. Rodney Clapp of Cascade Books has been a friend and colleague for over thirty years and with three different publishing houses. Thank you, Rodney, for seeing the merit in these essays and shepherding them through the publishing process.

Sometimes you need friends to look over your shoulder and tell you whether your hunches are worth following. When I compiled these chapters, I asked two friends to read them and tell me whether they thought that there was a coherent book here. Jim Armstrong and Joe Hum brought their respective experience in community development and Christian education to bear in reading these pieces. And they both confirmed that this was, indeed, a book, and encouraged me to bring this project to completion. If either of these wise friends had suggested otherwise, this book would probably not exist. Thank you, Jim and Joe.

This book is dedicated to my mentor, colleague, and friend Jim Olthuis. During my three years as a master's student at the Institute for Christian Studies (1976–1979), Jim modeled a scholarship of close and generous reading of other scholars, deep and sometimes wild creativity, and full-bodied passion. Jim taught me how to think Christianly in service of justice and love. If this book is about formation, then it is fitting that it should be dedicated to someone who has had such a profoundly formative influence in so many lives. I owe to Jim my greatest intellectual debt, and so much more.

All of these chapters had a previous life as presentations to various groups and their own publishing history.

ACKNOWLEDGMENTS

Chapter one: "Of Prophets, Priests, and Poets," was a farewell address to the Christian Reformed Campus Ministry Association upon my retirement in 2020 and was posted at Empire Remixed.[1]

Chapter two: "Transformation: Dynamic Worldview or Repressive Ideology?" was first published in the *Journal of Education and Christian Belief* 4.2 (Autumn 2000).

Chapter three: "Thinking 'Christianly' Revisited: A Dialogue" was first published in *Catalyst* 33.4 (April 2007).

Chapter four: "Education for Homelessness or Homemaking? The Christian College in a Postmodern Culture" was co-authored with Steven Bouma-Prediger and published in *Christian Scholar's Review* 32.3 (Spring 2003). It then appeared in *Taking Every Thought Captive: Forty Years of the Christian Scholar's Review*. Edited by Don King. Abilene, TX: Abilene Christian University Press, 2011. Copyright © 2011 by Christian Scholars Review. Used by permission of Abilene Christian University Press.

Chapter five: "Meredith on the Subway: A Story of Displacement and Homemaking" began as an article in the Dubuque University journal, *Character and . . . the Places of Home* Volume 4 (2018). The piece was further developed and revised for a presentation to the Outreach Conference of the Anglican Diocese of Toronto on October 28, 2023.

Chapter six: "Poverty, Justice and the Fruit of the Spirit," was a sermon for the Wine Before Breakfast community on August 20, 2013, and was posted at Empire Remixed.[2]

Chapter seven: "Faithfulness and Justice: Reformed Faith in the Face of Empire" was a Reformation Day sermon for Classis Toronto of the Christian Reformed Church on October 25, 2015, and was posted at Empire Remixed.[3]

---

1. https://empireremixed.com/2020/06/08/of-prophets-priests-and-poets-reflections-on-the-calling-of-campus-ministry/.

2. https://empireremixed.com/2013/08/26/poverty-justice-and-the-fruit-of-the-spirit-2/.

3. https://empireremixed.com/2015/10/26/faithfulness-and-justice-reformed-faith-in-the-face-of-empire/.

ACKNOWLEDGMENTS

Chapter eight: "On Not Forgetting Who You Are: A Targum" was initially written for my online class, "Colossians Revisited," at Bible Remixed in the fall of 2024, and was first posted at Empire Remixed.[4]

I acknowledge my debt to all of the audiences who have responded to this material over the years and the journals and books in which some of these chapters first appeared.

---

4. https://empireremixed.com/2024/11/06/a-targum-on-not-forgetting-who-you-are/.

Introduction
Christian Formation at the Gates of Hell

I once engaged in an abrasive act of NIMBYism. I willingly participated with a large group of neighbors in a "not-in-my-backyard" demonstration against some folks who had just moved into the area. We wanted to tell these newcomers, in no uncertain terms, that they were not welcome here. This was an act of radical inhospitality for which I offer no apology.

Here's what happened. In the early 1980s a group of people who openly and loudly identified themselves as members of the Ku Klux Klan set up shop in a house in the largely working-class Riverdale neighborhood of Toronto. A group of us who were in the same church got wind of this and immediately gathered the local churches together for a "Ban the Klan" march and rally. We had enough of our own white supremacist groups in Canada without importing the KKK from the United States. While we were generally known as community builders and activists for inclusivity, hospitality, and neighborliness, we decided that paradoxically such values required us to engage in an act of exclusion, inhospitality, and clear opposition.

After marching by the house, and having the Klansmen come out in their robes to shake their fists at us, we gathered for a rally in a local park. And, to show that our demonstration of exclusion was precisely in the service of a welcoming inclusivity, we hosted speeches and performances from a lot of folks from different groups: labor groups, feminist organizations, the LGBTQ community, the anti-apartheid movement (remember the date was the early 1980s), reproductive rights activists... they were all there. I was glad, and maybe even proud in a mildly self-righteous way, of the diversity of our rally, but as things unfolded I began to feel a little uneasy that no one from the church community had yet spoken. We were, after all, the organizers of this event. When would the voice of the church be heard? And maybe I was also becoming a little uncomfortable about the predominant "whiteness" of the proceedings. I mean, we were opposing a racist organization and yet no one from the Black community had taken to the stage. But finally, an African-Canadian woman from one of the churches was invited to address the crowd.

I don't remember her name or the name of the church, but it was something like "Sister Bernadette" from "The Apostolic, Holy Spirit, Church of the Holy Prophets, for the Last Times." And I was nervous. What was this wacky Black preacher lady going to say? I mean, she wasn't from a "reputable" church. She likely wasn't educated at one of the seminaries. What was she going to do? Was she going to get up there and start preaching her version of apocalyptic, Holy Spirit-filled, hell-and-damnation sermons? Was she going to embarrass us respectable and "progressive" church leaders with something too evangelistic? And the answer was, yes, she was going to preach, she was going to go down the path of hellfire damnation, and she was definitely going to be evangelistic.

And I can tell you, all these years later, exactly what she said. It was a sermon of incredible power and amazing brevity. It maybe took three minutes. With all of the rhetorical flourish and delivery style of a classic Black preaching tradition she proclaimed:

When Jesus came to Caesarea Philippi, he asked his disciples, "Who do men say I am?"

And they replied, "Some say John the Baptist, and others that you are a prophet."

"And who do you say I am?"

"You are the Christ, the Messiah of God," answered Peter.

And Jesus said, "Peter, the Holy Spirit has revealed this to you. And you will be the rock upon which I will build my church. And the

INTRODUCTION

GATES OF HELL WILL NOT PREVAIL AGAINST THE CHURCH OF JESUS CHRIST!"

Sister Bernadette then looked out at the crowd in that park and said, *"And I'm here to tell you that the Ku Klux Klan are the gates of hell and they will not prevail against the church of Jesus Christ."*

With that reverberating through a crowd stunned to silence, Sister Bernadette walked off the stage. Nothing else needed to be said. She confirmed my fear that she was going to preach the gospel and in doing so with such power, this woman convicted me of my sexism, cultural elitism, and racism. The very sins that I sought to exorcise from our community by participating in a "Ban the Klan" march and rally were deeply alive in my own heart, my own biases, my own worldview. I was trying to ban something from my neighborhood that had taken up comfortable residence in my own life.

I mark that event as among the most transformative moments in my life. Sexism, classism, and racism are demons that cannot be exorcised simply with a dramatic change of heart. These are ideologies rooted in vices that take deep hold in human life and culture. They are deformations of the human heart that require deep transformation and reformation.

That afternoon, at a "Ban the Klan" rally, I heard one of the very best sermons of my life. The gospel was proclaimed with a clarity that directly addressed not only the scourge of the kind of violent racism and white supremacy that is at the heart of the KKK, but also reached deep into the soul of a young man seeking to live a life of integral Christian discipleship, yet who was still burdened with the sinful biases of his culture and his privilege.

When Sister Bernadette proclaimed that "the gates of hell will not prevail against the church," she was employing the King James translation of this text. Most English translations, however, render the phrase as, "the gates of Hades." The forces of death will not prevail against the church precisely because the church is a resurrection community, a community of new life. Just as death could have no ultimate power over Jesus, so also does it have no final power over his body, manifest in a community of deep discipleship to this Jesus. Another way to put this would be to say that

INTRODUCTION

the principalities and powers in dark places, the demonic forces of anti-Creation in all of their ideological guises, throughout history, will not prevail against the church of Jesus Christ, rooted in and formed by the One who is the Life, the sovereign Lord of all things, who defeats death in resurrection and disarms the very forces of death that would seek to hold us all captive (Col 2:15).

Sister Bernadette knew all about captivity. She knew all about the forces of death that would hold her people in slavery. She knew all about the alarming number of young Black men who had died on the streets of Toronto and throughout North America. And, in the name of Jesus, she wasn't going to put up with it. In the name of Jesus, she would name the KKK, and all other racist movements, all other agents of oppression, violence, and exclusion, as the forces of death that they are. In the name of Jesus, she would name these movements, these perpetrators of death, as nothing less than "the gates of hell," that will not prevail against the church of Jesus Christ.

I have taken great comfort and courage in that sermon over the years. But now . . . well now, the sermon creates a painfully disquieting thought: what if the gates of hell *have* prevailed over the church of Jesus Christ? Or worse, what if the church *is* the gates of hell? What if we are experiencing yet again what Luther called "the Babylonian captivity of the church"? What if the church has fallen into such apostasy and become so complicit in ideological forces of death that the gates of hell have been opened wide?

Or maybe I should be more careful in what I am saying. Maybe we should not identify the whole church of Jesus Christ with the evangelical subculture in America. Maybe we should be more specific. Maybe the question is, what if the white evangelical church in the United States is the gates of hell? In light of the rise of Trumpism over that last number of years, we need to ask whether the church has once again been taken captive by a false gospel, an ideology and vision of life that is radically counter to that of Jesus. How else can we make sense out of 80 percent of evangelicals voting for a racist? How else can we make sense out of evangelicals openly embracing a white Christian nationalism that makes common cause with the Ku Klux Klan? How else can we make sense of evangelical leaders endorsing a misogynist and sexual abuser? How else can we make sense of such a large segment of the church embracing a creation-destroying ideology? How else can we make sense of embracing a politics of retribution, xenophobic hatred, and strongman autocracy by people who name Jesus as their Lord? Did Jesus seek retribution or offer forgiveness? Did Jesus promote hatred or was love at the center of his gospel? Did Jesus come as a pagan ruler to lord it over his subjects, or did he come as a servant who said that the first must be last?

From where I sit, it certainly looks like the gates of hell have prevailed over the church of Jesus Christ, or at least a disturbingly large portion of the church. And the tragic irony is that all of this is disastrous for the very "evangelism" that is at the heart of the name "evangelical." I have spent most of my ministry career addressing what some of us have come to describe as Post Evangelical Traumatic Stress Disorder (PETSD). It seems to me that this condition is now among us in epidemic proportions. The Babylonian captivity of the church has taken a Trumpian turn in our times that will bear the bad fruit of bringing scorn and disrespect on the gospel of Jesus Christ while leaving countless believers suffering from PETSD. And that can be a terminal condition resulting in the death of one's faith.

And so, we could say that Christian education and ministry at a time like this is all about Christian formation at the gates of hell. The chapters in this book were not initially conceived in these terms, but Sister Bernadette's prophetic word so many years ago, updated in terms of the apostasy that we have seen take hold in recent times, serves to helpfully frame the themes that I have addressed over the years and continue to address in this book.

The opening chapter, "Of Prophets, Priests, and Poets," was presented to colleagues in campus ministry upon my retirement in 2020, in which I offered a reflection on the shape of my ministry over the years. Set in the context of a pastoral ministry, especially among those suffering from PETSD, I reflect on the power of prophetic teaching and preaching to deconstruct ideological distortions of Christian faith while inviting folks into the liberating story of God's redemption of all things. That invitation, however, must come with two things: the ministry must be a place where we come together in healing and restoration; and our captivated imaginations must be transformed by meaningful and poetic liturgy.

Such a ministry for transformation has been at the heart of my work since Richard Middleton and I published *The Transforming Vision* forty years ago. That book on shaping a Christian worldview went on to have an illustrious career in multiple translations. But "worldviews," even transformational worldviews, are not immune to ideological distortion and captivity. Just witness how the language of worldview is employed among Trumpian Christians today. In the second chapter of the present book, "Transformation: Dynamic Worldview or Repressive Ideology?" I address this question by outlining the way in which even the rhetoric of transformation can be reduced to ideology.

While chapter 2 also begins to address how a deeply biblical worldview might resist the temptation to ideology, the overall direction of my thought towards questions of virtue and character formation begins to get teased out in the third chapter, "Thinking 'Christianly' Revisited: A Dialogue." What if we moved away from the intellectualism that has so often plagued discourse around the integration of faith and scholarship by taking the character ethic that Paul so powerfully evokes in the third chapter of his epistle to the Colossians and applying it to the whole question of knowing? What if things like compassion, kindness, humility, meekness, patience, and love were taken to be epistemological virtues? What would Christian scholarship look like if it was rooted in the peace of Christ, suffused with gratitude, and offered as an act of worship? Would the gates of hell have such easy access to such scholarship and the kind of community that it engenders?

The fourth chapter, co-authored with Steven Bouma-Prediger, frames the whole practice of Christian education in terms of the deeply biblical metaphor of home. What is Christian education for? What kind of people do we seek to form through our educational ministries? Specifically addressing the calling of Christian higher education, we ask whether our educational institutions are offering an "Education for Homelessness or Homemaking?" In this experimental essay, Bouma-Prediger and I take our cue from leading agrarian thinkers Wes Jackson, Wendell Berry, and David Orr, by promoting a fundamental redirection of education towards homemaking. Might such an educational agenda serve to deconstruct the xenophobic home of American exceptionalism, reconstructing it precisely in the direction of social, cultural, economic, and ecological homemaking for hospitality?

Chapter 5 returns to themes of character and virtue, and it illustrates what such educational focus on homemaking looks like by telling the story of "Meredith on the Subway." In this story of displacement and homemaking we meet a young woman who engages in courageous acts of defending her neighbors against the forces of exclusion, and we reflect on just what was it in Meredith's formation that shaped her to be the kind of person that she is.

Since we could sum up so much of what we mean by the formation of Christian character, the virtues of homemaking, and even the shape of Christian knowing, by reference to the virtues that are born of the gospel, it makes sense to include a sermon on the fruit of the Spirit. Chapter 6, "Poverty, Justice, and the Fruit of the Spirit," reads the famous list of Galatians 5:22–23 as virtues rooted in the story of Jesus that shape the public praxis and witness of the church. If Jesus is right when he says that "you will know them by their fruits" (Matt 7:16) then we need to be intentional about evaluating the faithfulness of the church not so much by intellectual assent to certain doctrines, but by the way in which our communal life together bears the fruit of the gospel.

This leads us to another sermon, and the seventh chapter of this book: "Faithfulness and Justice: Reformed Faith in the Face of Empire." If we understand the Reformation as (among other things) a liberation of the church from its Babylonian captivity through a fresh reading of Scripture, then how might we read Scripture in the context of our own imperial captivity to set us free? If the Reformation principle of *Ecclesia semper reformanda est* ("the Church must always be reforming") continues to hold, and if it is true that the church is called to be in a constant process of reformation in changing cultural and geopolitical contexts, then how do we hear Scripture in a way that sets us free from the ideological captivity that surrounds us, and, as I noted in my story about Sister Bernadette, is deep within each of us?

As this book was coming to completion in the fall of 2024, Donald Trump was re-elected as the President of the United States. The questions of Christian formation and praxis that are my concern in these essays became all the more acute. The weekend before the election I wrote a targum on Colossians 3:1–17. This revisitation of a text that we have already engaged in chapter 3 of this book picks up on the practice of writing expansive paraphrases of biblical texts that Sylvia Keesmaat and I have done in our books *Colossians Remixed: Subverting the Empire* and *Romans Disarmed: Resisting Empire/Demanding Justice*. A targum attempts to rehear an ancient biblical text as if it were written to us, just the other week. What might Colossians 3 sound like if Paul was writing to us with this particular election on the horizon? And how might this text resonate with us, indeed, shape our character and our response at this moment in history? I offer "On Not Forgetting Who We Are: A Targum" as the final chapter of this book.

So, perhaps we could say that this book is about Christian formation at the gates of hell. Rooted in a lifetime of educational ministry, these are, if you will, dispatches from the front. Bolstered by Sister Bernadette's prophetic word so many years ago, and with a sober assessment of the challenges to authentic Christian faith in our time, I offer these reflections in service of a ministry of Christian formation that liberates us from our cultural captivity and sets us free to a path of radical and healing discipleship.

1

Of Prophets, Priests, and Poets
Autobiographical Reflections on the Calling of Campus Ministry

INTRODUCTORY COMMENTS

Upon my retirement from almost twenty-five years serving as a Christian Reformed campus minister at the University of Toronto, I was invited to present something of a farewell lecture for a conference of colleagues. When I came up with the title—"Of Prophets, Priests, and Poets"—I was alluding to the dedication of my first book with Sylvia Keesmaat, *Colossians Remixed*.[1] That book was dedicated to my (now late) friend, Bud Osborn. Bud was a street poet and fearless advocate for the poorest of the poor in the famed Downtown Eastside of Vancouver. Bud was a prophet, priest, and poet, and he had a profound impact on my life.[2] So I thought that I could put together a bit of a manifesto, a radical vision of campus

---

1. Walsh and Keesmaat, *Colossians Remixed*.

2. A good start in reading Bud Osborn would be *Hundred Block Rock* and *Keys to Kingdoms*.

ministry, a rallying call to my colleagues—something fitting for a farewell lecture—all under the categories of prophets, priests, and poets. But then I remembered that I have an aversion to vision statements and manifestos; I also remembered that I have always been reticent to speak to my campus ministry colleagues in a way that might suffer from the presumption that I have something to say that folks don't already know.

The more I thought about this presentation the more it became clear that the subtitle was missing one crucial word: autobiographical. These are not so much words of wisdom that the retiring campus minister imparts to his younger colleagues as they are autobiographical reflections on the calling of campus ministry. And the triad of prophets, priests, and poets serves me well in sharing these reflections. So, I'd like to go to the beginning of my story and share two life-changing events of my very early Christian discipleship.

TWO LIFE-CHANGING EVENTS

While the most life-changing event of my life was coming to be a follower of Jesus sometime in fall of 1969, there were two other events that happened within about a year and a half of my conversion that were foundational to the shape of my discipleship and ministry. One was a large conference and the other was a small meeting. As I look back upon these two events, I can see how profoundly formative they were in my life. And both events had everything to do with campus ministry.

Some fourteen months after my conversion, a man gave my grandmother some money so that her young grandson, recently converted to Christian faith, could attend the InterVarsity Christian Fellowship Urbana Missions Conference between Christmas and New Years of 1970/71 at the University of Illinois. At that conference, four things deeply resonated with my young faith and had a profound impact on my calling in life.

The first was that I got to listen to the great biblical expositor John Stott give four evening Bible studies on the Upper Room discourse in the Gospel of John. I had been converted just a little more than a year earlier reading the Gospel of John, and here was a man with a winsome intellect and a profoundly deep faith taking us deeper and deeper into that intimate conversation between Jesus and his disciples on the eve of his betrayal, arrest, trial, and crucifixion. Now, I didn't have a "when I grow up I want to be John Stott" kind of experience, but I certainly had a sense that if I was going to open the Scriptures for people as part of my calling, then Stott had set the standard. Not that I would mimic Stott's expository style, or even come to the same exegetical conclusions as this great Bible teacher, but that my engagement with Scripture, and my calling as an expounder of the word, would need to strive to be as winsome, as faithful, as engaging, and as intelligent as what I saw displayed those four evenings at Urbana.

The second thing that happened at that conference was that I met American racial tension in the flesh for the first time. The African American preacher and civil rights advocate Tom Skinner gave a talk called "Your God Is Too White." You couldn't get anywhere near the stage because all the Black kids showed up an hour early to grab all the seats at the front. And the tension in the room was palpable. I was a very young white Christian convert boy from Canada, and here was an event addressing matters of race that threatened to undermine much of the evangelical theology and church culture that I had experienced in that first year of discipleship. I knew that there was something very right about the Black kids being at the front with their backs to the dominant white audience behind them.

Tom Skinner's talk began to dismantle what was an implicitly (and often enough explicitly) racist kind of Christian faith, and my path towards a lifetime of seeking a socially engaged, radical discipleship was solidified by my third experience at Urbana. The Latin American Christian leader Samuel Escobar gave a lecture that introduced us to something very new in the world of Christian thought and practice: he offered us an evangelical version of liberation theology. Here was a faith with justice at its core. Here was a Christian discipleship that recognized that the preferential option for the poor wasn't Marxist rhetoric, but gospel truth. Here was a hermeneutic that released the Scriptures from their pietistic and individualistic shackles, allowing the liberating power of the gospel and the radical praxis of Jesus to deeply transform our lives.

All that happened at Urbana 70 for me. And it all happened from the main stage. But there was one other thing going on at that conference that was kind of an underground, subversive, and decidedly unsanctioned movement. Every day a newspaper was being handed out that commented on, and often critiqued, what had happened at the conference the day before. It was called *The Vanguard*, and it was clearly more radical than anything that IVCF would sanction. Articles outlined the connections between evangelical missionary activity around the world and the forces of American imperialism. After Skinner's talk the editors of this guerrilla movement interviewed all the mission agencies at the conference to see if they actually welcomed Black folks to be missionaries. The vast majority did not! They published this news, and the dormitory where the Black kids were segregated exploded. (Yes, the registration form asked you to identify your race, and the Black kids were in separate dorms from everyone else.)

We all wanted to know: who were these people behind *The Vanguard*? What was their agenda? Why were the organizers denouncing them from the stage? Why did their stuff sound so right, even though it all seemed somewhat dangerous? Now here is the interesting thing: I wouldn't find out who these radicals were for another three and half years until I stumbled into the Christian Reformed campus ministry at the University of Toronto. This guerrilla vanguard of radical discipleship was connected to the Institute for Christian Studies (ICS), a graduate school based in Toronto, and a whole bunch of these folks worshiped with the CRC campus ministry. When I found that community in 1974, I had a deep sense of homecoming. I went on to do my master's degree at ICS, then served on staff before joining the faculty from 1987 to 1995.

At this post-retirement stage of my life, I need to testify that those four things—Stott's biblical exposition, Skinner's anti-racism gospel, Escobar's liberation theology, and a bunch of radical Reformed students and faculty stirring up the pot—pretty much set me on the path that I've been on in discipleship, scholarship, writing, and campus ministry for the last fifty years.

But, there was one other little event that shaped me. Sometime in that early period of following Jesus, while I was still in high school, I got invited to an IVCF meeting at the University of Toronto. And there, this seventeen-year-old convert hung out with much more mature Christians that were in their early twenties. At this meeting an IVCF staff worker—I can't remember who it was—gave a talk. I don't remember what it was about, but I knew that it was good. This guy had a group of some twenty-five or thirty students hanging on his every word. Listening to him unpack the Scriptures, prod the students with questions, and begin to discern what Christian faith looks like in a modern university, I knew what I wanted to do with my life. When I grew up, I wanted that guy's job. I wanted to spend my life unpacking the Scriptures, helping to dig deep into the struggles of life, accompanying students into more radical paths of discipleship. Yep, the youngest kid in the room, the kid who wasn't even at university yet, figured that his life would somehow be bound up with campus ministry.

So here is the first thing that I want to tell you in this chapter that you already know: campus ministry changes lives. Whether it is in a local meeting of a campus fellowship group or in a large public event, whether it is sanctioned by the church or is an underground guerrilla movement, campus ministry changes lives. In deep gratitude and joy, I want to bear witness that those experiences of campus ministry at very early moments of my Christian life profoundly formed me, gave me a vision, and made a call on my life. And one way I could describe that call would be to talk about prophets, priests, and poets.

OF PROPHETS . . .

For whatever reason, there was a prophetic edge to some of my earliest and most formative experiences of Christian faith. While many young Christian converts in the late sixties were cutting their hair and burning their rock and roll albums, my conversion resulted in long hair and an abiding love and interest for contemporary music.[3] For me, the Jesus who I met while reading the Gospel of John and hanging out at a soup kitchen mission in the inner city of Toronto was radically countercultural, in constant conflict with the authorities, wouldn't play by the rules of the dominant class, and gathered around him an alternative community rooted in the values of the kingdom, not the empire.

So when I stumbled into the CRC campus ministry at the University of Toronto and actually found such a community who followed this radical Jesus, I was all in. In that community I began to come to a deeper understanding of the prophetic tradition and how it is at the heart of campus ministry.

Here's the thing about the biblical prophets. They were creative and courageous leaders of intellectual rigor, liberated imagination, and cultural discernment who were deeply rooted in the Scriptures of Israel. Such theological depth and breadth of vision sounds to me like campus ministry at its best.

Let's begin with depth. The prophets engaged in a ministry of retrieval and remembering for an amnesiac people who had lost their way. The prophetic word only sounded novel and new because the people had forgotten their own story; they had lost the plot, and their imaginations had been taken captive by alien, and invariably idolatrous, cultural systems, symbols, and narratives. The prophets' radical words served to remind the people of who they were, where they came from, and what the shape of covenantal faithfulness looked like.

Such a prophetic ministry of retrieval and remembering helpfully characterizes campus ministry.[4] Isn't that why teaching is at the heart of such a calling? We seek to open the Scriptures in

---

3. Manifest in my work on U2, "Wake up Dead Man," and "Walk On"; Bruce Cockburn, *Kicking at the Darkness*; and Leonard Cohen, *Rags of Light*.

4. Deeply informative for this understanding of the prophetic voice is, of course, Walter Brueggemann's whole body of work. Especially foundational has been *Prophetic Imagination*.

our campus ministry communities precisely because we know that without deep roots in the story of God with God's people and all of creation, we will lose the plot of the gospel and forget who we are. One way to describe this is to say that our evangelistic and pastoral ministry is one of inviting folks into the story of Jesus. To do that we need to be constantly digging into the story: engaging Jesus in the Gospels, understanding how the Torah and prophetic literature, along with other writings, shaped the kingdom worldview in Jesus, and following that narrative through the discipleship of the Acts of Apostles, the epistles to the early church, and the other writings in the New Testament.

This is a ministry of remembering that retrieves what has been lost. In terms of my understanding of the distinctiveness of campus ministry within a broadly Reformed perspective, this is crucial. Forgive me if this sounds harsh, but it seems to me that a lot of Reformed folks have sold their birthright for a pottage of evangelical pietism. Rooted in the sacred/secular, heaven/earth, soul/body dualisms that have taken the Christian imagination captive for most of our history, this kind of pietism (found in so many campus ministries and perpetuated in most of our hymnody) seems so pious with its Jesus talk, but in fact it leaves the church wide open for cultural captivity. Once you have split the world up into two realms of sacred and secular, once you have named heaven as your escape destination away from earth, and once you have divided the human person into a soul and a body, Christian faith becomes at best irrelevant to embodied, earthly, cultural reality. At worst, it becomes a pious legitimation of idolatrous cultural practices, systems, and patterns of life.

In principle, a Reformational understanding of Christian faith knows better. And thus, my entry into campus ministry was through teaching Christian worldview courses on secular campuses. In these classes we wrestled with pivotal questions: how can we break through the dualisms that have held us captive for so long and embrace a holistic worldview, a transforming vision of all of life? How might we read Scripture that would release it from the shackles of such dualism? How might we have the audacity of an Abraham Kuyper and confess that there is not one square inch of all of creation over which God is not lovingly and redemptively sovereign?[5]

If it is true that there is something prophetic about this kind of teaching, then we should not be surprised when such exposition of a biblical worldview creates tensions and crises in our midst. How many times have I heard a student raised in the church exclaim, *"Why didn't anyone tell me this stuff in my church? Why do I have to unlearn so much of the piety and theology of my church background if I am going to really engage the Scriptures and follow a path of radical discipleship? Do you know what happened at Thanksgiving when I started talking about this stuff at the dinner table? A big theological argument erupted!"*

It is, therefore, not surprising that campus ministers, who are employees and servants of the church, often find ourselves, like the prophets before us, creating trouble in and for the church. It is very hard to be a court prophet. But there is a sense in which campus ministry is called to precisely such prophetic ministry. Living and working at the margins of both the academy and the church, we are mandated, I believe, to be a prophetic voice calling those around us to a deeper fidelity, a more radical faithfulness, a more holistic and liberating worldview. Our prophetic calling is to be bold but not arrogant as we negotiate our service to the church, subject to our higher and more radical calling to the kingdom of God.

Given this prophetic emphasis on biblical depth and an integrative worldview, it is no wonder that campus ministries within a Reformed tradition have been known for the breadth of their vision. If we are doing this kind of prophetic teaching ministry on campus, and if this is a vision that anticipates nothing less than the redemption and reconciliation of all things (as Paul puts it in Colossians 1:15–20), then surely we must be all about tracing the connection between this comprehensive vision of life and the crucially important work of scholarship and education in the modern university. No wonder such campus ministries are well known and respected for their emphasis on the integration of faith and

---

5. Found in Bratt, ed., *Abraham Kuyper*, 488.

academic studies. We might not have always known what we were doing, but if we are proclaiming a gospel of such cosmic scope on the university campus then undoubtedly we would want to help students and faculty to develop an integrally Christian perspective in their work at the university. Without question, this has been hard work; this has been a struggling-with-principalities-and-powers kind of work. So much is at stake for both students and faculty to "play the game," to learn the paradigms of their disciplines, and to not ask embarrassing questions in the academic sphere, especially if they are "religious" in character.

You see, the dualistic distortion of Christian faith serves the academy well. If scholarship is scientifically objective and therefore religiously neutral, then students and professors alike learn to leave their religious assumptions at the door. But the genius of Reformed faith, and one of the most significant contributions of the Reformed tradition to Christian scholarship around the world, has been to debunk and deconstruct this false dichotomy. So, employing the best resources that Reformed scholars (and others) have produced over the last half-century, campus ministers have sought to encourage integrative scholarship through their ministries. My own approach was to try to keep on top of the Christian scholarship in any given field just enough so that I could ask good questions. I didn't presume to prescribe what "*the* Christian perspective" would be in any given field, but I wanted always to be able to find the right questions that would probe into the core issues in a field of scholarship. The strategy wasn't a matter of making dogmatic pronouncements but rather of creating a community of communal discernment in which the hard questions could be raised. Indeed, if at the end of a conversation more questions were on the table than when we began, I would take that to be a sign of success.

Of course, one of the problems with this approach was that it seemed to privilege "scholarship" when most of our students had no intentions of becoming scholars per se, but were instead seeking an education towards various kinds of occupations. That is a fair and important critique. Most students just want to get their degree and get a job and they don't have the time, inclination, or disposition to get into the worldview issues at stake in any given discipline. Nor do they need to. But what all students do need is to reflect on what Christian discipleship looks like in the totality of life. And surely an integrally biblical campus ministry should be fundamentally directed towards precisely such discipleship. If a student has the privilege to engage in post-secondary education, then they are on a path of cultural, professional, and community leadership. And the same principles and questions that we would struggle with in the faith/learning kind of discussion apply to the issues of leadership development in any other field. In campus ministry we try to form communities of discipleship to help students thrive at college or university precisely so that they will be shaped into deeply and radically Christian cultural leaders in all of life: from vocation to family to church to sexuality to politics to ecology to economics, to literally every area of life.

That provides a segue to one more thing to say about the prophetic nature of campus ministry. The prophets knew that justice was at the heart of the Torah. "Justice, and only justice, you shall pursue," insists Deuteronomy (16:20). "What does the Lord require of you," writes Micah, "but to do justice, love kindness, and walk humbly with your God?" (6:8). "Let justice flow down like a mighty river," thunders Amos (5:24). The deeper you get into the biblical story the more deafeningly the bells of justice ring. This too should be at the heart of any campus ministry that would stand in the tradition of the prophets. And when justice becomes the lens through which you engage the world, all kinds of new questions emerge about vocation, family, church, sexuality, politics, ecology, and economics. So often our students receive a justice education in the context of campus ministry that is alien and often even oppositional to what they have learned at home and in their churches. I have had more than one student say to me, with a chuckle and gratitude, that campus ministry ruined their lives because we opened them up to a vision of justice that meant that the comfortable path that they were on now had to be abandoned and a new, more difficult, but also more exciting, path of discipleship needed to be embarked upon.

When you understand the call to justice, you become painfully aware of both your own privilege and your complicity in injustice. Your eyes are opened to a wounded world of oppression on the brink of collapse or self-implosion. Your ears are unstopped and you hear the cries of the most vulnerable, the discarded, and the despised. I think you begin to see the world more through the swollen, tear-filled eyes of Jesus. And if such a vision proves true, if the preferential option for the poor that liberation theology discerns in the biblical witness is accurate, then might it not also entail what we could call "the epistemological priority of suffering"? What happens if we prioritize suffering in our engagement with the world? How does an attention to suffering—be it ecological or socio-economic hardship, or those under the burden of mental illness or sexual discrimination—shape our understanding of the world and how we will live into radical discipleship in the conflicted and compromised realms of vocation, family, church, sexuality, politics, ecology, and economics?

It seems to me that the breadth of campus ministry, especially if it has profoundly biblical depth, calls us to shape prophetic communities of justice-seeking discipleship on our campuses, for the sake of the university, for the sake of the church, and for the sake of the world that God sent his only Son to redeem.

But, of course, all of this requires more than just prophets. We also need priests.

OF PRIESTS . . .

All of this talk about the prophetic calling of campus ministry can be quite heady. Biblical theology, Christian worldview, faith/learning integration, all of life redeemed, cultural engagement, pursuing justice in the face of systems of oppression—maybe there is something about the seriousness of the Reformational intellectual tradition that gives us a proclivity to such large ideas and agendas. But with such heady ideas comes the danger of Reformed folks replacing a dualistic pietism with an intellectualism that is no less dualistic. This is the kind of thing that Jamie Smith has been critiquing in his cultural liturgies project.[6] We abandon a culturally compromised pietism only to embrace a different kind of dualism between the mind and the body. Many of us live a lot in our heads, but faith is always embodied and experienced in the midst of real, conflicted, compromised, suffering, and confused lives.

That means that there is an indispensable priestly character to campus ministry that must complement and ground the prophetic dimension of such work. Some campus ministers are better at the priestly side of things than others, and that is one very good reason to have team ministries in which different gifts are manifest in the leadership. But the point isn't so much a matter of finding folks with a priestly gift as it is to live into our communal calling as a royal priesthood. The church is called to be a priestly community mediating the grace of God to the world even as it holds the pain of the world in its heart.

I have loved my ministry of teaching, preaching, writing, and being something of a theological provocateur, but I've got to tell you that the moments of deepest honor for me as a campus pastor were always pastoral. Engaging in a ministry of accompaniment through the dark valleys in students' lives; a ministry of listening and encouragement; praying with someone and reminding them that they are beloved, forgiven, and gifted—these are when I feel like I have entered the holy of holies. Sometimes these are awful, tragic, heartbreaking moments of sorrow. I have buried three babies. I have witnessed the dissolution of marriages. I have been in the psych ward to visit suicidal students. I have pastored those weighed down with sorrow and exhaustion. At other times, these pastoral moments are ones of such unspeakable joy—a baptism, a reaffirmation of faith, moments of healing, milestones in students' lives, and I've lost count of the how many weddings I've conducted.

Times of joy and times of sorrow. In sickness and in health. In good times and bad times. This coming alongside one another is at the covenantal heart of all ministry, not least of all campus ministry. It has been especially important in my ministry that we have been a place where lament is welcome. My experience is that

---

6. Smith, *Desiring the Kingdom*; *Imagining the Kingdom*; *Awaiting the King*.

students are looking less for answers and more for authenticity. In the context of a church that prioritizes and perhaps even mandates "joy" there is something liberating about a community that can give painful and sometimes abrasive voice to lament. Walter Brueggemann is right: "only grief permits newness."[7] Indeed, grief is the doorway to hope, and you don't get to real hope without going through that doorway. My experience of campus ministry is that, when deeply authentic, it is bathed in grief. Moreover, holding a space for that grief is integral to our priestly calling; holding and creating space (and time) for grief, for lament, and for sorrow in pastoral conversations and worship liturgies without trying to fix anything, allows leaders and students to support each other and draw closer to God. In fact, that "holding space" is what transforms our offices and meeting areas into sacred spaces. Somehow a space needs to be baptized by tears before it can be holy. I think that our campus ministry office at the University of Toronto was one of the holiest places on campus.[8]

But there is another "holding" that I perceive in the priestly dimension of our calling. I would call it the "holding of faith." I said earlier that campus ministers don't have all the answers, but they should have a good collection of questions. It is also true that campus ministers don't have all the faith, or a final angle on the faith, or even a consistently strong and secure faith. But we are people of faith, longing to grow in faith, and to shape a community of faith. And I think that we have the high calling of holding faith for those who cannot.

Let me explain it this way: so many of the people who end up in a campus ministry office or at a campus ministry service are taking their last shot at Christian faith. They are the "dones"— "been there, done that, got the Christian T-shirt, and I can show you the scars." So many of the folks I encountered suffered from Post-Evangelical Traumatic Stress Disorder (PETSD). They can't quite believe anymore, not in the way they had before, but there is

---

7. Brueggemann, *Hopeful Imagination*, 41. See also his *Reality, Grief, Hope*.

8. I have reflected further on how our office was a sacred space in my essay, "Sacred Space."

something about a campus ministry community that attracts them for one last shot at staying in the story. And the gift of a campus ministry community is that it can hold the faith and embody the story for these folks who are in the midst of what is often a painful transition. The community holds the story, struggles to live in the story, and in doing so we keep the story alive for others to explore as they discern whether they want to stay or get into the story themselves. Agnostics, atheists, and folks from other religions are all welcome. We hold the story, but not too tightly, lest it becomes our possession and we refuse to welcome others.

To extend this more personally, I think that sometimes in pastoral care we are called to hold faith, or hope, for someone else. Does a student think that she is so broken that she is not worthy of God's love, and could not possibly receive forgiveness? Well, I can simply assure her that while she cannot believe in God's love for her, I as her pastor am happy to hold that belief on her behalf. Or perhaps a marriage is in crisis, and you know that a crucial counseling session is coming up on Friday; well, you can intentionally hold the pain of that relationship, bearing both spiritually and physically that pain through fasting and prayer on the day of that appointment. Holding space, holding faith, holding pain, holding hope—these, I believe, are integral to our priestly calling.

Now, let me say something about poets.

OF POETS . . .

Any discerning reader has not been surprised that Walter Brueggemann's work has appeared a number of times in this chapter. At times I think that much of my writing is an extended footnote on what I have learned from Brueggemann about reading Scripture in the context of late modern culture. So, you won't be surprised by this quote: "the key pathology of our time, which seduces us all, is the reduction of the imagination so that we are too numb, satiated and co-opted to do serious imaginative work."[9] Faithful cultural

---

9. Brueggemann, *Interpretation and Obedience*, 199.

engagement, embodying the gospel, enacting the story of redemption in all of life—in our families and churches, in our sexuality and gender identity, in our political lives and ecological care, in our economic lives and occupations—requires serious imaginative work. It isn't simply a matter of believing certain things and then putting them into practice, because if we have reduced or captive imaginations, then we simply won't have the resources of imagination to envision what faithful life looks like.

Again, Jamie Smith's cultural liturgics project proves to be helpful. Humans are liturgical animals, writes Smith, "who live off the stuff of imagination: stories, pictures, images, and metaphors are the poetry of our embodied existence."[10] Embodied existence, real life at your place of employment, in the polling booth, going to church, doing the shopping, or raising kids, is rooted in and reflective of the stories, pictures, images, and metaphors that shape our imaginations. Because of this, I have spent the last twenty-five years of my ministry focusing on the poetic—not in the sense of writing poetry, but in the sense of what my friend Amanda Jagt describes as "a linguistic style that touches our lived experience and opens our imaginations through the art of wordplay."[11] And this has brought me to a more poetic form of liturgy that "can unveil resonances between different texts, themes, and images, introducing them to our imaginations."[12] The Wine Before Breakfast community that began one week after the catastrophic attacks on September 11, 2001 and ran until the summer of 2023 was an experiment in imagination.[13] Attending to the poetic shape of worship, prayer, and music, we sought to be a community of Christian imagination. We wanted to open the word in such a way that Scripture breathed and moved within us. We engaged in contemporary music in our liturgies not

10. Smith, *Imagining the Kingdom*, 126.
11. Amanda Jagt, personal correspondence (October 29, 2024).
12. Again, from Amanda Jagt, personal correspondence (October 29, 2024).
13. Two books emerged out of the Wine Before Breakfast community. Brian J. Walsh and the Wine Before Breakfast Community, *St. John Before Breakfast*, and *Habakkuk Before Breakfast*. Many sermons and reflection pieces that emerged out of this community can be found at Empire Remixed, https://empireremixed.com/.

to seek relevance but to hear the resonances: how does the artist's imagination resonate with a biblical imagination, especially with the text(s) of the day? How does one open up the other? And how are our imaginations shaped in the interface? Through the poetics of liturgy, and centrally in the imaginative enactment of the narrative through the concreteness of the Eucharist, we found our imaginations opened up and liberated for radical discipleship.

If our worship is going to liberate our imaginations, then it will need to be profoundly biblical, symbolically rich, culturally engaged, unafraid of lament and pain, deeply eucharistic, and so honestly authentic that it will simply not put up with bullshit. Now here is the thing. Almost all of the prophetic literature of the Bible is poetic; the priestly language of the Psalms is equally poetic. So, I am saying that if campus ministry is to be prophetic and priestly, then it will necessarily also be poetic.

NO MANIFESTO, JUST A TESTIMONY

This essay offers no grand manifesto for campus ministry. It is just a testimony. I felt a call to campus ministry very early in my Christian life, and it was an amazing gift that I was able to live into that calling. Over the years there were times when I was blown away that I got paid to do what was so close to my heart and calling. At the University of Toronto I was blessed with wonderful colleagues who brought their own gifts to our team ministry.

The Wine Before Breakfast community was as much a place of healing and homemaking for me as it was for the hundreds of folks who were formed in our midst and who in turn shaped our community. Especially meaningful to me was the music, for there is no poetics without music. Sometimes I joke that I founded Wine Before Breakfast just so I could have a place to hear my musical friends play at 7:22 on Tuesday mornings. That is mostly true. My gratitude to the bandhood of all believers is immeasurable.

I began this chapter by talking about my late friend, the poet, priest, and prophet Bud Osborn. I will end with one of his poems, which is also a prayer, called "Down Here." With abrasive and strident poetic rage, the poem depicts the lives of the most oppressed and broken people in our society.[14] It ends with these lines:

> let my words
> sing a prayer
> not a curse
> to the tragic
> & sacred mystery
>
> of our beautiful
> suffering
> eternal worth

Let it be so.

---

14. Osborn, "Down Here," from *Keys to Kingdoms*. Steven Bouma-Prediger and I engage this poem in some depth in the Postscript to *Beyond Homelessness*, 330–33.

2

Transformation
Dynamic Worldview or Repressive Ideology?

ON THE WRITING OF WORLDVIEW BOOKS

When Christians talk and write about education, the discourse of "transformation" is often nearby.[1] Christian education, if it is to be worthy of its name, must be transformational in character. And, as Christian educators, we root our transformational view of education in a biblical worldview. We are concerned with transformation not because a modernist narrative of the ineluctable progress of humanity animates our work, but because we believe that in Christ all things are made new. And we believe that such newness in Christ is not a once and for all accomplishment in the life of an individual, but an ongoing dynamic in history and in all of creation.

1. For example, consider Andrew Wright's, "Transformative Christian Education." See also Hobson and Welbourne, "Conceptual Basis." It is important to note, however, that the language of "transformation" is not exclusive to Christian discourse in education. Consider O'Sullivan's profound reflection on education in a period of cultural decline, *Transformative Learning*.

We need to be transformational in education because the transforming vision of the biblical worldview is a vision that responds prophetically and creatively to each new situation. Now I don't drop a phrase like "the transforming vision" just to be self-referential. Some readers of this chapter will know of the book that Richard Middleton and I co-authored some forty years ago, entitled *The Transforming Vision: Shaping a Christian World View*.[2] Richard and I have been amazed, gratified, and deeply humbled by the impact that this little book has had in the Christian community, especially in the area of education. The book has had a life and a ministry that goes far beyond anything that its authors ever anticipated.

As Richard and I have talked to people over the years about the book, we have often asked them how the book functioned in their lives. What kind of book was this for them? How did they receive it the first time they read it? And we have found some categories developed by Walter Brueggemann to be helpful in understanding the various ways in which the book has impacted people. Specifically talking about the Psalms, Brueggemann distinguishes between three different kinds of psalms—psalms of orientation, disorientation, and reorientation.[3] And it seems to me that these categories are helpful in talking about other kinds of texts as well. Some texts function as *orientation* texts for us. They are texts that tell you how things work, how things basically hang together in life. They are orientation texts because they provide us with a basic orientation and foundational direction for life.

Other texts are more *disorienting* in character, either because they are giving painful voice to a sense of disorientation or because in our reading of these texts we get disoriented. The psalms of lament that scream at God to wake up and get involved again in the calamities of his people, and moreover blame God for those calamities, give voice to a disorientation that says things are not working out here, we can't make sense of reality anymore.[4]

2. Walsh and Middleton, *Transforming Vision*.
3. Brueggemann, *Message of the Psalms*.
4. Psalms 44 and 88 are good examples of such abrasive lament. They not

Thirdly, some texts could be described as texts of *reorientation*. You get a sense when you read them that the author has come through a process wherein a previously settled orientation has been turned on its head; the author has struggled through a period of deeply painful disorientation but has now come to a profound resolution of the previous time of troubles and has experienced a liberating reorientation. In the psalms, such reorientation is often articulated in terms of singing "a new song."

So, some texts orient life, some disorient things, and others are read and experienced as a breakthrough to a renewed orientation. Interestingly, Richard and I have found that *The Transforming Vision* has been a text that has taken on all three roles in people's lives. Some folks read that book and it precipitated a profound worldview crisis for them. Our non-dualistic interpretation of Scripture, together with our appraisal and critique of Western modern culture, served to undermine deeply held and previously unquestioned beliefs. Disorientation was the result.

Others picked up the book and had an almost immediate "aha" kind of experience. They reported back to us that what we managed to do was to articulate precisely what they were struggling with and provide them with a new, transformational way of living and thinking. For them, this was a reorientation text.

But the text also functions as an orientation text for people. Indeed, it is often people who first experienced reorientation in this book that then, after a few years, became so comfortable with this vision of Christian discipleship, this "transforming vision" way of reading Scripture and engaging culture, that the book essentially became a text of orientation in their lives. My hunch is that this is the predominant way the book functioned in the area of Christian education. And there is nothing surprising about this. In many ways *The Transforming Vision* is fundamentally a book of orientation. In the book, Richard and I attempt to give the lay of the land and provide a foundational perspective or orientation that

---

only give voice to a time of deep disorientation, they also create a sense of disorientation when they are read. Maybe that is why the lament psalms are read so seldom in our churches!

will help Christians navigate their way as disciples of Jesus Christ at the end of the twentieth century (neither of us thought that the book would still be in print in the twenty-first century!):

> Here is how a worldview works as a vision of and for life, formed, articulated and enacted in community.
> Here is how worldviews take on cultural flesh.
> Here is the basic shape of a biblical worldview: creation, fall, and redemption.
> Here is what got the church off the tracks: dualism.
> Here is the way in which Western culture, rooted in such a dualism, developed into the kind of idolatrous culture in which we presently live.
> And here is how to engage that culture in general, and academic life in particular, in a way that is biblically faithful.

So, in writing a book like this, we attempted to give orientation, direction, a sense of bearings, and a foundational framework for a transformational Christian discipleship. Forty years, multiple translations, and countless printings later, however, I perceive there to be a problem. In fact, there are two problems. The first is a problem with worldviews. The second is a problem with disorientation.

THE PROBLEM WITH WORLDVIEWS

Over the years a lot of Christian scholars have offered a critique of the very notion of worldviews. In education, Nicholas Wolterstorff has been vocal for decades on the limitation of worldview language to describe what Christian education is all about. Wolterstorff is worried that worldview is too "viewish" and not concerned enough with praxis. We need to raise children not just to think Christianly, but to live Christianly; that is, we are called to an education for discipleship, for praxis.[5] Richard and I had no difficulty with Wolterstorff's insistence on praxis in education, and we felt

---

5. See especially Wolterstorff's *Educating for Responsible Action*, together with Stronks and Blomberg, eds., *Vision With A Task*.

that such an emphasis was always at the heart of what we were striving for in *The Transforming Vision*.[6]

Others are more taken by the postmodern critique of worldviews.[7] Think about it for a moment: worldviews are, after all, *world*views. They are, by definition, comprehensive in scope; they are integrating perspectives addressing all of life; they place things in the broadest possible horizon; they determine who is in and who is out, what is right and what is wrong. They are, in short, prime examples of what postmodernists call "totality thinking."[8] And all such attempts at totality, postmodernists insist, must be deconstructed as the ideological power grabs that they are. They claim to be universal, but are necessarily the particular perspective of a certain time and place. They claim to be comprehensive, but can only do so by marginalizing and ruling out of order any and all alternative visions. And such worldviews hide their own constructed character behind a facade of either the rhetoric of common sense ("don't all thinking people see things this way?") or the heavy hand of divine sanction ("this is the Christian worldview! It is simply what the Bible teaches if you would only open your eyes to see it!"). It is this last strategy of legitimation (the heavy hand of divine sanction) that has so many Christian scholars and educators reacting against the discourse of worldviews. It is all too heavy-handed, there is no room to move, to change, to grow, to question. For them, the rhetoric of education and scholarship directed by a Christian worldview is a cover for an imposed orthodoxy. "The Christian worldview" becomes the fence that keeps you penned in and inhibits creativity. There may well be the rhetoric of transformation, but the reality is that there is an imposed uniformity and sameness. Educationally, such an employment of worldview

---

6. It is worth noting that Professor Wolterstorff honored us by writing the Foreword to the book.

7. Most trenchant, however, in critique of the intellectualism of worldview discourse is, of course, James K. A. Smith's cultural liturgics project already noted in chapter one of this book.

8. Keesmaat and I address the question of totality thinking with specific reference to reading the epistle to the Colossians in *Colossians Remixed,* esp. ch. 6.

discourse serves to engender schools of protective custody rather than dynamic transformation.

THE PROBLEM OF DISORIENTATION

There is, however, a second problem with worldview talk that I think is even more pressing, at least at an existential level. If you read the psalms of disorientation you will be able to discern that the problems there expressed are often not just that the prior orientation is no longer sufficient, but that there is, more devastatingly, a sense that the psalmist's present crisis is not taken seriously when placed in the context of that orientation. I can illustrate this with reference to Job. Job's life falls apart and he can't figure out why. His experience was in profound tension with the orientation that he had come to accept as covenantal Jewish faith. If he was God-fearing and Torah-obeying, then why does all hell break loose in his life? How can he deal with this disorienting tension between prior orientation and present experience? Enter his friends. "There is no disjunction, no tension. The prior orientation said that if you sinned, life will fall apart. Your life has fallen apart. Ergo, you must have sinned."

Do you see what is going on here? Job's complaint, his lament, his disorientation is dismissed by his friends in the name of the orthodoxy of their shared Jewish orientation in life. Job's disorientation is not taken seriously and he is counseled to stop questioning, accept the answers that an orthodox worldview provides, repent, and get on with life. Job will have nothing of it. And, as far as I can see, young people in a post-Christendom age will have nothing of it either. Imposing upon their experience the dictates of a previously articulated worldview, even if that is the articulation of a transformational worldview, will invariably result in alienation, rebellion, and rejection.

Perhaps another metaphor could help us get at the problem. Worldviews are often described as maps that provide orientation and direction. But how helpful is a map when you are so disoriented that you can't even find where you are on the map, or when it is too dark to even read the map? Canadian singer-songwriter Bruce Cockburn's perspective on maps needs to be taken seriously by anyone preoccupied with worldviews:

> Sometimes the best map will not guide you
> you can't see what's round the bend
> sometimes the road leads through dark places
> sometimes the darkness is your friend
> today these eyes scan bleached out land
> for the coming of the outbound stage
> pacing the cage[9]

In the "bleached out land" that characterizes the cultural wilderness of late-modern or postmodern culture, we still need vision, we still seek to find a way forward and perhaps even escape, but sometimes the best maps will prove to be insufficient. Indeed, sometimes it feels as if it is precisely these maps, these worldviews, these comprehensive frameworks, that have caged us in, and puts us to pacing, impatient for our freedom.

So here is the question that arises out of this problematizing of worldviews. If it is true that sometimes maps will fail us and perhaps even imprison us, and if there is some truth in the postmodern critique of worldviews as invariably repressive power grabs under the cover of either common sense or biblical sanction, then what do we do with our own rhetoric of transformation? Or to put the question more simply and starkly, can a transformational worldview—even one that is deeply rooted in Scripture—become a repressive, closed-in-on-itself ideology? If it is in principle possible that any orientation can easily become a self-justifying ideology that will not countenance disorientation and therefore can never give birth to a reorientation, then could this be happening in our own worldview, our own educational practice, our own lives? Sadly, I think that the answer to this question is yes.

---

9. Bruce Cockburn, "Pacing the Cage," *Charity of Night*, 1996.

FROM DYNAMIC WORLDVIEW TO REPRESSIVE IDEOLOGY

It seems to me that there are five ways in which a biblically rooted, transformational worldview can succumb to ideology. And these five ways, my five points, just happen to produce an interesting acronym that some readers might recognize: TULIP. Only here, TULIP has no direct reference to the so-called five points of Calvinism as encoded by the Synod of Dordt, but refers to the five components of a worldview turned ideology.[10] In summary, worldviews become ideologies when they become:

> *Total* Systems of
> *Universal* Finality that have
> *Lost* their Biblical Dynamism, thereby becoming
> *Inconsequential* and *Irrelevant* to changing cultural contexts, because they are preoccupied with the
> *Protective* Ethos of an enclosed community

Let's unpack this is some detail.

Total Systems

A transformationally dynamic worldview can be reduced to a repressive ideology if it is taken to be a *total system*. The problem that I am identifying here is an overemphasis on a legitimate dimension of all worldviews. Worldviews are visions of life that

---

10. For the non-Calvinist readers of this chapter a word of explanation is in order. In 1618–19 a synod was convened in the Dutch city of Dordrecht to deal with the heretical doctrines of Jacob Arminius. Arminius had five points of doctrine that the synod deemed heretical and in need of rebuttal. The form of the rebuttal came in five counterpoints that were summarized in twentieth-century appropriations of that synod's conclusions by the acronym TULIP. Those points are: Total depravity, Unconditional election, Limited atonement, Irresistible grace, and the Perseverance of the saints. Even though that summary fails to capture the nuances and complexities of Reformed faith (which the Synod of Dordrecht was not attempting to accomplish in its deliberations), for the purposes of this chapter, the acronym TULIP is useful on a number of levels. See Billings, "Problem with TULIP."

are comprehensive in scope. Any worldview must be a *world*view, addressing all of life. Consequently, worldviews make real cognitive claims about the world that are, moreover, invariably set in the context of a grand story or metanarrative. And while the postmodern incredulity toward all metanarrative is perfectly understandable given the career of every metanarrative on offer (including the Christian one), it seems to me that metanarratives are, to put it plainly and simply, an essential dimension of human life and culture-forming.[11] The problem, however, is an overemphasis on this comprehensive character of worldviews and the way in which this dimension of worldviews gets articulated and thought through. What happens is that we end up with worldviews that function as cognitively overloaded totality systems. In education this results in an intellectualism that bears little formative fruit in the lives of our students, engenders an unseemly intellectual arrogance and superiority complex amongst its adherents, and privileges only the cognitively gifted in our classrooms.

The problem with worldview as a total system is that this model fails to recognize that no worldview ever attains a *total* perspective because all worldviews are located in particular times, cultures, and traditions. There is no such thing as a timeless worldview.

More importantly, however, the notion of worldview as total system buys into an intellectualism that says that if we think right we will act right. You know the argument: "If only we get our intellectual categories straight then we will live in terms of those categories." The problem is that there is no evidence whatsoever that this might in fact be the case. Again, this is why Wolterstorff is so critical of the limitations of education for forming a "Christian mind." The problem is that "minds" are only one dimension of what it means to be human and what inspires and directs human action. My fear is that we have so over-intellectualized our worldview that our imaginations have been taken culturally captive.[12]

---

11. Richard Middleton and I have argued this more fully in *Truth is Stranger*, esp. chapters 4 and 5.

12. See my *Subversive Christianity*, esp. ch. 2.

Another way to put this is that while systems can be taught, worldviews are caught. Systems are prone to catechetical instruction and affirmation. Worldviews capture your heart and imagination. Systems tend to be static and timeless. Worldviews are dynamic and historically situated. This leads me to my second point.

Universal Finality

A worldview is on the path of ideology when it is taken to represent *universal finality*. Again, this problem emerges from an overemphasis of a legitimate dimension of all worldviews. Worldviews are never the private possession of local communities. I'm not sure that anyone really believes that their worldview is fine for them, but not necessarily for everyone. Even the relativist thinks that others should be relativistic. The tolerant liberal refuses to tolerate intolerant conservatives. All worldviews implicitly or explicitly make truth claims of universal applicability, and they make those claims with a faith-directed certainty.

But when you hold a worldview with universal finality—that is, with the belief that this worldview has arrived at ultimate and universal truth, with no need to listen and learn from any other worldview—then an ideology has been born. With the pretense of universal finality is lost a proper grasp of the particularity, ambiguity, and unfinished character of one's own vision.

Lost Biblical Dynamism

A third way that a transformative worldview can succumb to ideology is when it loses its *biblical dynamism*. (Admittedly, I'm stretching my language in order to make my acronym work!) The kind of transformational worldview that has animated so much of Christian educational theory and practice has its vitality, its power, its depth of insight, its grounding in Christ only to the degree that it is constantly informed by, corrected, and revisioned by a dynamic engagement with Scripture. The danger is that once our worldview has been transformed by a more holistic and perhaps more radical way of reading Scripture, we again think that we have arrived. The temptation is that either its authors or its readers think that a book like *The Transforming Vision* got it all right.

In such a context I would suggest that we always follow this hermeneutical rule: If our reading of Scripture always confirms our worldview and if the Scriptures never surprise, confuse, upset, or disorient us, then we are undoubtedly misreading the Scriptures. A sure sign of ideology is when the Bible only functions as a text of orientation in our lives. If this text never disorients us, then it will never have the resources to provide us with reorientation in changing and confusing cultural contexts.

There is another dimension of this loss of biblical dynamism that merits comment. One of the consequences of an ideological worldview and an ideological approach to the biblical text is that paradoxically the text tends to lose its currency in our lives. Moreover, I have observed that many of those who talk long and loud about biblical authority seldom find it necessary to deeply engage this text. You can see how this works. Once you think that you know what the Bible says, all that is left is to proclaim the authority of the Bible ever louder. You don't have to actually read the text or struggle with it because you already know what it is going to say. Sadly, however, what is really proclaimed as authoritative is not the Bible but the ideological worldview that we impose upon this text.[13]

With the loss of biblical vitality, not only does the worldview become repressively ideological, the community also succumbs to biblical illiteracy. And when that happens, the death of the church and the various ministries and cultural expressions of the Christian community, including the Christian school, is not far behind.

---

13. Lest the reader think that I am constructing a straw man here, I will name names. Ronald Nash's *Worldviews in Conflict* presents itself as a defense of Christianity in the world of ideas. Apart from this succumbing to the intellectualistic temptation critiqued above, it is instructive that this defense and exposition of a Christian "worldview" has no need to ever actually engage the biblical text with any exegetical attention. Moreover, the author also doesn't find it necessary to devote more than a few sentences to Jesus!

Inconsequential and Irrelevant

A fourth indication that a transformational worldview is devolving into an ideology is when that worldview becomes inconsequential and irrelevant to its changing cultural context. For a worldview to sustain people with a vision and not be reduced to a set of catechetical affirmations, it must engender a transformational praxis. As soon as a worldview becomes ideological, its cultural witness becomes locked into a particular time and place, thereby losing its ability to maintain a radical and prophetic relevance to changing circumstances.

The relation between worldviews and cultural praxis is two-directional. Not only is cultural praxis rooted in some kind of worldview, worldview is always lived and formed in interaction with cultural praxis. The intellectualism that so often characterizes ideologically constricted worldviews gives rise to this kind of cultural irrelevance precisely because worldview conformity or adherence is measured in terms of intellectual assent to certain doctrines rather than by the praxis of the worldview-shaped community.

Some years ago, a graduate student wrote to me about a doctoral dissertation that he was writing on the effectiveness of Christian colleges in inculcating a Christian worldview in their students. He had set up a survey that he was sending out to alumni of one Christian college as part of his research, and since he was, at least in his own mind, so indebted to the influence of *The Transforming Vision* in his work, he asked me if I would comment on the survey he had designed. The immediate problem was that the survey asked questions that, given the context, had clearly right and wrong answers, which would render the results useless from a social scientific perspective. For example: "Do you think it important to pray for your colleagues at work?" What Christian college grad would want to say no to that?

But there was another glaring problem with the research that was foundational to this student's dissertation. When it came down to it, all he was doing by means of this survey was measuring what these people *thought* about the world, not how they actually lived.

This student felt that if he could ascertain the basic furniture of the intellectual framework of these alumni, then he would be able to discern the effectiveness of their Christian college education.

I wrote back and suggested that the student had not understood what worldviews were all about and that this survey would not give him real insight at all. I suggested a different kind of survey that would ask different kinds of questions. Things like . . .

> What kind of involvement do you have in your neighborhood?
>
> What are the local social and political issues that you are concerned with?
>
> How do you enact that concern?
>
> Would you please send us a photograph of your living room? [Which could then be analyzed in terms of the art on the wall, whether there is a television or video game console, etc. in the room, and how the furniture is set up in relation to such entertainment technology.]
>
> Could you estimate for us how much time you spend watching television each day? How much time surfing the net or on social media?
>
> Would you send us a list of your favorite television shows and websites?
>
> Could you please send us a list of the meals you have shared with your family in the last two weeks? What was on the menu?
>
> Where do you buy your groceries?
>
> What is your principal means of transportation?
>
> Would you be so kind as to send us your last three credit card statements?

> Would you give us permission to sift through your garbage at the side of the road for the next three weeks? We promise not to make a mess, we just want to see what kinds of things you throw out.

I suggested to this doctoral student that if he wanted to know about the Christian worldview of these Christian college alumni, then these would be the kinds of things that might help him make such a discernment. Worldviews are lived more than they are thought. And the question of the success of Christian education hinges on the lived lives of our graduates. The issue for Christian education must be character formation for radical discipleship.

The first time that I ever attended a meeting about Christian education, someone asked whether the children from this school would be able to "fit in" to the larger culture when they graduated. And I'll never forget the answer that the principal of that school gave. "Fit in? I certainly hope not! We are educating these children to be misfits for the kingdom of God." And by this she did not mean that these would be people who couldn't engage their culture because they had been sequestered into a closed-in-on-itself tribal community. Nor was she envisioning a militant Christian nationalism that would seize political power and control of the judicial system. Rather, she sought an education that would help these children to be fully engaged in their culture, living out of a radically different vision, animated by an alternative imagination rooted in the deepest values of Christian faith such as love, forgiveness, justice, compassion, and peace. This was an education that was consequential because it was relevant. And it was relevant because it refused to allow its own worldview to be reduced to an intellectualistic ideology. This leads me to my fifth point.

Protective Ethos

A transformational worldview becomes ideological when it is employed to serve a *protective ethos* of safety in a self-enclosed Christian community. A protective ethos that seeks to insulate our children and ourselves from the world rather than forming character that will engage the world with the love of Jesus manifest on the cross, is an ideology that is unworthy of the gospel and Christ's sacrifice.

Similar to my comments about total systems and universal finality, there is something legitimate about worldviews functioning to create an ordered world of some safety. One can be secure in the faith and at home with Jesus. And a biblical worldview does (like all worldviews) create something of a sacred canopy over us.[14] But that secure structure is, in biblical tradition, always open to deconstruction when it serves a self-protective community with a fortress mentality. Biblical faith is clear on this. The secure home of covenantal life before the face of God is not for self-enclosed protection but for ministry. This home is characterized not by the locked doors of ideological fear but by the open and risky hospitality of a community that is open to the world because it confesses that Christ died for this world.[15]

The offense of a richly biblical worldview is that it offers us comfort and security only by taking the yoke of Christ. But this yoke turns out to be a cross of suffering service. This is not a safe worldview compared to how most people understand safety. And when a worldview becomes preoccupied with safety, together with matters of purity and keeping oneself unstained by the world, then it is clear that a dynamic worldview has become a repressive ideology.

So, can a dynamic, transformational—even deeply biblical—worldview succumb to ideological distortion? Yes, of course it can—especially when that worldview is taken to be a *total system* of *universal finality* that *loses its biblical dynamism*, thereby also becoming *irrelevant and inconsequential* to changing cultural contexts precisely because it is *preoccupied with a protective ethos* of an enclosed community. And if our schools seem to be such enclosed communities driven by a fearful and reactionary protective ethos,

---

14. This was a central insight of Berger's *Sacred Canopy*.
15. Bouma-Prediger and I develop a phenomenology of home, with serious consideration of the relation of boundaries to hospitality, in *Beyond Homelessness*, ch. 2.

then I would humbly submit that such schools are more likely rooted in a repressive ideology than a dynamically biblical worldview.

KEEPING A DYNAMIC WORLDVIEW DYNAMIC

While the temptation to ideology is strong, it is not inevitable that worldviews succumb to ideology. So, in conclusion, I will offer some suggestions on how a dynamically biblical worldview might be able to remain transformational. And I will make my suggestions in reverse order to the five points just enumerated, though I will make no further attempt to work with the TULIP acronym. We've already pushed that as far as it will go (and likely further!).

Hospitality

If a sure sign that a worldview has become an ideology is when that worldview serves to legitimate an exclusive and self-enclosed community animated by a *protective ethos*, then a dynamically biblical worldview is formative of a community characterized by hospitality. Parker Palmer says that "hospitality means receiving each other with openness and care."[16] Hospitality is the opposite of fearful protectionism. And an educational community that is rooted in the gospel of Jesus Christ, a gospel characterized by fellowship with sinners, tax collectors, prostitutes, and the unclean, must be a community that dares to risk similar fellowship in our own very different context. A community formed and continually reformed by a radically biblical worldview is secure enough in the power of love, reconciliation, and grace—indeed, in the power of its Lord—that it dares to risk hospitality to people of other faiths and other worldviews, and it dares to risk hospitality to ideas, issues, and questions that might make members of the community

---

16. Palmer, *To Know as We are Known*, 73. A comprehensive and evocative study of hospitality in the Christian tradition is Pohl, *Making Room*. A creative application of the theme of hospitality to education, specifically foreign language teaching is found in Smith and Carvill, *Gift of the Stranger*. See also Smith, *Learning from the Stranger*.

uncomfortable. Indeed, it is precisely through such risky hospitality that a worldview is often kept open. This leads to my second point.

Prophetic Imagination

Ideology is such a devastating betrayal of a transformational worldview precisely because it becomes culturally *inconsequential*. Most of us were drawn to transformational ways of living and thinking, however, because this seemed to us to be a more culturally attuned and relevant expression of Christian faith. If we are to maintain and foster the continued vitality and dynamism of such a transformational worldview, then, our worldview and the educational manifestations of that worldview must be driven by a passionate and *prophetic imagination* that has the courage and the creativity to engage a changing cultural reality. This does not mean that we seek relevance for the sake of relevance. Rather, we will engage in a dynamic cultural and educational praxis that will be subversively relevant to the cultural and educational ideologies of our time. This is a prophetic imagination because it seeks to engage in prophetic discernment and critique and to raise up Christian young people with such a discerning spirit. And it is a passionate imagination both because it cuts through the numbness of late-modern and postmodern culture and because it is an imagination driven and directed by a God who loves the world so much that he gives his only Son to die for that world. Ours is a passionate imagination because we are subjects of a king who was enthroned on a cross.[17]

Dynamic Biblical Engagement

All of this means that one sustains a dynamically biblical worldview only through a *dynamic engagement with Scripture*. Biblical reflection is foundational to all of Christian life, education included. But this requires an ongoing serious, passionate, and loving engagement with Scripture. And this must be an engagement that

---

17. See Wright, *Jesus and the Victory*, especially chapter 12 (sections 5, 6, 7).

allows our reading of Scripture to be full of questions and to be patient enough not to demand answers too quickly. The Bible as an easy-answer-book-of-theological-orthodoxy, or quick-manual-of-moral-absolutes, or compendium-of-timeless-truths is, I suggest, the first step to ideology and a lost biblical dynamism. What we need is an indwelling of the biblical narrative in such a way that this story, with all of its tensions, plot confusions, and dead-ends, and in all of its historical oddities, is, nonetheless, our story. The word of Christ "dwells in us richly" (Col 3:16) only when we embody that word in our lives, when we find our identity as the people of God in this narrative, and when this dynamic word shapes our character and forms our vision.

An Interpretive Community

Moreover, we need to remember that a community formed in such a way by the word is, by definition, an interpretive community. Yes, we are a biblical community and we want to root our lives in a biblical worldview, but the Bible is a book, and books require interpretation. It is, therefore, highly inappropriate that we should ever claim universal finality for our worldview. Such finality is impossible when it comes to interpretation. We need to acknowledge that worldviews, and the interpretations on which they are based, are not handed down complete from heaven. Rather, interpretation is something people do in community, in relation to tradition, and in a particular time and place. And that means that worldviews are in fact constructed in community and in history.

The worldview that Richard and I articulated in *The Transforming Vision* is timed. It was rooted in a Dutch Reformational tradition that we had come into contact with at the Institute for Christian Studies in Toronto.[18] It was formed and developed in a Canadian context during the Reagan administration in the United States. It was written by two guys who were pretty sure of themselves, and who listened to a lot of Bruce Cockburn, etc. The worldview that

18. Our understanding of worldview was also, of course, deeply influenced by studying with James H. Olthuis. See his "On Worldviews."

was articulated in that book forty years ago was a construct. It was a way of thinking, a way of being, a way of viewing the world and living in that world that was constructed at a particular time and place. And we do well to never forget that constructed character of worldviews. It keeps us from ever concluding that our worldview represents universal finality, it keeps us open to other worldviews and their insights into God's creation, and it keeps us humble.

Forming worldviews is part and parcel of our call to be stewards of God's good creation. You can't be a steward of a garden, or a city, or a culture—all of which are changing over time in history—without a worldview, a grounding and guiding orientation. And just as we must never absolutize any agricultural, cultural or civilizational form, so also must we never absolutize our worldview constructs. Rather, we attempt to be faithful in all that we do—including our formation of a worldview. And since the world has not come to universal finality, neither can our worldviews.

An Ongoing Story

Finally, I began this whole discussion by saying that when a dynamically biblical worldview is taken to be a total system, we invariably find ourselves on the path of ideology. It is, therefore, important that we remember that a biblical worldview is, at heart, not a system at all; it is an *ongoing story*. A biblical worldview is a storied vision of and for life. Worldviews are always rooted in story and "if a story is to remain vibrant and formative, there must be a community of people capable of remembering and reinterpreting that story." Only then is the community "capable of ordering their new experience in a manner consistent with their story."[19] But

---

19. Fernhout, "Christian Schooling," 86. Fernhout is dependent here on Hauerwas, *Community of Character*. N. T. Wright offers a helpful rethinking of the idea of worldviews as invariably rooted in story, embodied in praxis and encoded in powerful symbols in *New Testament and the People of God*, ch. 5. Bouma-Prediger and I employ this model to understand the relation of housing to homemaking in *Beyond Homelessness*, ch. 4, and Keesmaat and I use the same model to describe the contrast between the worldviews of ancient Rome, the earliest Christian community, Indigenous peoples in Canada, and

therein lies the rub. A storied vision of and for life, a narratively formed worldview, can only remain vital if that story is adaptable to changing historical conditions. The story requires fresh reinterpretation if it is not to become a dead tradition. Sylvia Keesmaat puts it this way: "When tradition is handed on unchanged it loses its potency and has little meaning for the present. Some would go so far as to say that an unchanged tradition is dead, it has been killed. The only way for a tradition to be fertile and alive is for a transformation to occur."[20]

So how can we guard against a transformational worldview becoming an ideology? By so indwelling the biblical narrative of suffering love that we not only allow, but expect, our transformational worldview itself to be continually transformed.

---

late-modern/postmodern culture, in *Romans Disarmed*, ch. 3.

20. Keesmaat, *Paul and His Story*, 20–21.

3

Thinking "Christianly" Revisited
A Dialogue

So, I've been asked to write an article on "thinking Christianly."
Oh yeah? So do a riff on "fides quaerens intellectum" ("faith seeking understanding") for a few pages and you're there.

Well, that's a possibility, but there are some problems with that.
Problems? What problems?
When we say that faith seeks understanding, the question that comes to my mind is, "understanding what?" What is it that faith seeks to understand?
Itself, of course. Faith seeks maturity and deepening by means of coming to an understanding of itself. Isn't that what theology is all about?

Yes, that is what theology is all about, but I'm not always so sure that such a theological enterprise, even under the rubric of "faith seeking understanding," contributes that much to Christian thinking.
I'm not following you.

I guess that I'm wondering why we think that Christian thinking is limited to theological thinking. I'm wondering why the understanding that faith seeks is an understanding of itself.
What else could it be?
Christian thinking could be a way of thinking that permeates, shapes, and directs all of our thinking and all of our acting. The understanding that faith seeks could be an understanding of everything.

Look, I love theology, but if theology attempts to understand everything, doesn't it start to get too big for its britches? Doesn't it start to have aspirations of royalty all over again?
No, because this kind of thinking, this kind of understanding, isn't the unique and sole aspiration of theology. Theology has a servant role in helping the people of God to think Christianly, but thinking Christianly isn't a matter of thinking theologically. At least not in the narrower definition of theology as the academic study of the nature of God and the system of religious belief.

I'm still not getting it. If the character of our thinking needs to be Christian—even if it is about everything (though I don't quite get that either)—then how could it ever be Christian without theological deepening and direction?
I admit that I'm actually conflicted on this myself. I agree that thinking Christianly needs theological deepening and direction, but I'm decidedly under-whelmed by the ability of Christian theology—at least in the modern age, and from both more liberal and more conservative perspectives—to engender anything close to integrally Christian perspectives in areas like engineering, economics, social science, the arts, medicine, urban planning, and pretty much every other area of cultural endeavor.

Come on, there is a plethora of books out there dealing with all kinds of themes like these from a theological perspective.
Fair enough, and I don't want to overstate my case. Indeed, I rejoice in the veritable renaissance of Christian reflection on these

and many other areas of life. But I'm still uneasy with much of what I've read. So much of this literature amounts to little more than absolutistic pronouncements on God's view of things like the movies, philosophy, bioethics, and politics. There seems to me to be so little engagement in this kind of heavy-handed imposition of a Christian worldview.

Wait a minute, aren't you yourself one of those "worldview" guys?
Yeah, but sometimes I wish that I'd found another word to describe what I'm struggling towards. I'm convinced that an absolutistic worldview is always bad news and always fails to really engage the world.

Why is that?
Because an absolutistic perspective can't deal with the dynamism of a changing world. It gets reduced to a crabby contrarianism at best and a militant triumphalism at worst. Either be upset about the world around you or start strategizing to take the world over for Jesus. Neither option accords well with Scripture, I think.
Scripture? That's precisely what these folks insist they are resting upon! God's eternal, infallible and immutable word!

Immutable words can't take flesh.
Why not?
Because flesh mutates. Flesh grows, changes, sweats, moves in time. Flesh bleeds when it is pierced with nails. Immutable words don't bleed.
What?
Don't you get it? This view of Scripture, this kind of absolutism, has no flesh to it. It's got no balls!

WHAT?

I'm sorry, I know that it is impolite to refer to our Lord and Savior's scrotum—even if it is only metaphorically. But this is what I'm getting at. If we are going to think Christianly then we will need to do so from a place of engagement, of embodiment, a place of blood and suffering, of pain and disappointment, a place in time. Indeed, we will need to think Christianly from a place, from a location in the world. And if that location is to be Christian, if that location is to be where Jesus is, then it will need to be a location of suffering. It will need to be a location of powerlessness, not power. It will need to stand with Jesus on the margins, not at the center. Or if it is at the center, then it will likely be on trial for blasphemy and treason. If it isn't there, then I don't know how it can be Christian.

Kind of sounds like a liberationist perspective.
Perhaps it is. Perhaps we need to agree with liberation theology that not only does the gospel have a preferential option for the poor, but that this entails an epistemological privileging of pain. When Christian faith seeks understanding it goes to the cross, it goes to the places of oppression, injustice, and suffering. You see, if faith can't find understanding in those places, then it can't understand either itself or the world in which it is to be practiced.

And a Christian worldview and the Scriptures don't help with this understanding and this practice?
Of course they help. Without the Scriptures there is no understanding. Heck, there probably isn't any faith either. And I still think the Scriptures serve to shape a community's worldview. It's just that I think that an absolutistic worldview imposed on reality is neither biblical nor respectful of the reality on which it is imposed.

So what's the alternative?
This is going to sound trite, but maybe the alternative is to stop thinking so much and start being.

I can't believe you said that.
Neither can I. And I'm not trying to set up that tired old thinking/being dichotomy all over again. But I am trying to combat the intellectualism of most worldview thinking that seems to assume

that if we think right, then we will live right. There seems to me to be not one shred of evidence to support that assumption.

So again, what's the alternative?
We need to understand three things.

First, worldviews are narratively shaped. If we are going to retain the notion of worldview at all, then we need to sever it from an intellectualism whereby worldview is just a code word for what we used to call systematic theology. Worldviews have cognitive content, but they are not cognitive systems. They are storied visions of life, and the best way to be deepened in a particular worldview is by hearing, celebrating, and retelling the stories that are its foundation.

Second, worldviews—storied visions of and for life—shape us not so much by retooling our cognitive frameworks, but rather by capturing our imaginations. Perhaps that is the weakness of the overly visual metaphor employed in the term "worldview." What I'm getting at, and what I think cultural anthropologists like Clifford Geertz and Mary Douglas were getting at, is the way in which a worldview shapes how one feels, experiences, senses, responds, cares, and engages the world.[1] Maybe imagination helps us here. The issue isn't just how you "see" the world but also how your imagination shapes the way in which you construe the world. Not just *what* you see, but *how* you see it, *why* you see what you see, and what *hope* you have for what you see. Imagination isn't content with simply seeing the world as it is; it has the audacity to imagine that the world could be different.

That's two things, what's the third?
The third thing has to do with character and virtue. If we understand worldviews as storied visions of and for life, then the way that such a storied imagination shapes life is through the forming of character. By indwelling this story, by allowing this story to shape the identity of the community, we become certain kinds of people. We embody certain kinds of virtues in our lives.

---

1. Geertz, *Interpretation of Cultures*; Douglas, *Purity and Danger*.

Okay, I'm starting to understand where you are going with this understanding of worldview, even though you are now talking a language of narrative, character, and virtue that I would identify with people like Hauerwas who is decidedly anti-worldview.[2]
Yeah, well sometimes you end up with odd bedfellows.
I don't think I'll touch that one with a ten-foot pole
Good idea.

But I still don't see how this gets us much further with "thinking Christianly." Nor can I see how the Scriptures will function in all of this.
Well, let's consider Colossians.
Somehow I knew you would end up in Colossians. Do you think that Colossians can answer every question that we ask in the twenty-first century?
It's not a matter of this ancient text answering every question. Sometimes a close reading of this text helps us to raise new and different questions. But, yes, I think that the sheer scope of Paul's vision in Colossians shapes our imaginations in such a way that we have deep resources to engage our world, to live faithful lives, and even to think more Christianly.

Didn't you and Sylvia Keesmaat find a political ethic and even an ecological ethic in Colossians 3?
Yes, in *Colossians Remixed* we thought through the narrative ethic that Paul proposes, and we specifically asked how the virtues that he identifies with the new self in Christ—the character of Christian life—would play out in our political and ecological lives. I think we can do the same thing with the question of thinking Christianly.

If the virtues of Christian character rooted in the story of Christ crucified, buried, risen, ascended, and coming again (Col 3:1–4) can be understood to engender a political and an ecological ethic (Col 3:12–17), why not read these virtues again and imagine how they would shape an epistemology?

2. Hauerwas, *Community of Character*.

I thought you were pushing it when you found political and environmental ethics in the text, but this is clearly over the top.

Take a look at the text for second. If we are concerned about thinking Christianly, and if we want that kind of thinking to not be a narrowly intellectualistic exercise but a way of interpreting the world precisely to engender faithful praxis in that world, then Colossians just might be our text.

You've still got my attention.

Okay, so try this out. The comprehensiveness of Paul's vision of the gospel of Christ is undeniable in the letter.

True enough. In Christ "all things" have been created. He is "before all things," "in him all things hold together," he has "first place in everything," and "through him God was pleased to reconcile all things." The poem in 1:15–20 is clearly breathtaking in its scope.

And "all things" means "all things," right?

No argument.

Great. Now notice that Paul is also preoccupied with themes of knowledge in this letter. He prays that the Colossians will be filled with all knowledge, wisdom, and understanding (1:9); he wants to teach them in all wisdom (1:28) because in Christ is "hidden all the treasures of wisdom and knowledge" (2:3).

Yes . . . go on.

And when he makes the shift in chapter 3 from the vices of the empire to the virtues of the kingdom, he says that we have been clothed with the new self "which is being renewed in knowledge according to the image of its Creator" (3:10).

Yes . . . wonderful stuff. We are renewed in the image of God—renewed to our full humanity and our full calling as God's stewards in creation. I love it.

Amen. But notice that this renewal "in knowledge" is according to the image of the Creator. Exactly what is entailed in that

knowledge is something that I'm not sure we can unpack in this dialogue, but it includes things like knowledge of what God is up to in the world through Jesus—that is, a deeper knowledge of the narrative of redemption. And it also entails, I think, deeper self-knowledge of who we are called to be as God's image-bearers in a world populated by the false knowledge of idolatry.
Sounds good, but how does that help us to "think Christianly"?

The same way that it helps us live our political and ecological lives Christianly. Take a look at the virtues that Paul lists and ask yourself, what would my thinking, my imagining, my construing of the world, look like if it was shaped by these virtues?
You mean that list that includes compassion, kindness, humility, meekness, patience, forgiveness, and love in Colossians 3:12–14?

That's the list. Christians are shaped as people of compassion. How do such people think? How do such people know the world? When they look at the world, what do they see, and where do they look? *If compassion is a matter of sharing pain, then I would imagine that this would entail a knowing of the world through the eyes of pain.*
Yes, maybe we could call it a suffering epistemology. A way of thinking that is invariably drawn to where the blood is. A way of thinking that embraces the world in its suffering.

And what about kindness, humility, and meekness?
Maybe folks who embody these virtues are people who eschew an arrogant and aggressive epistemology of subjection and mastery precisely because they know the world through a humility that recognizes its own limitations, its own fallibility and finitude, and that takes a stance of receptivity to the world. Instead of an aggressive realism, such virtues call forth a listening epistemology in which our knowing of the world is a matter of epistemological stewardship. We are called to care for and tend the world through our knowing. We are called to interpret the creational glossolalia all around us, hearing the voice of creation in its joy and its sorrow.

I'm not sure that I really know what all of this means, but let's keep going. How about patience and forgiveness?
I'm not sure that I know what all of this means either, but wouldn't a knowing suffused with patience be the opposite of our culture of quick fixes and cheap answers? Wouldn't patience entail a slower, more careful attention to the world, one which takes the time to foster an intimacy in our knowledge of the world? And wouldn't a forgiving spirit suggest a more communal, less individualistic, more relational, and less antagonistic approach to knowledge?
That might change the nature of debate in church and academy, in politics and business.
Yeah, and maybe in our domestic feuds as well.

It all comes down to love, doesn't it?
That's not too surprising, is it?
No, not when you consider that the Hebrew word for knowledge is the same as the word for sexual intimacy.
Or that the Hebrew word for truth is the same as the word for fidelity, or troth. And that while Paul wrote in Greek he still thought in Hebrew.

This reminds me of N. T. Wright's take on epistemological love.[3]
That's right (no pun intended). To know is to love. Knowing Christianly is a knowing that affirms the reality and goodness of the other, and longs to enter into a covenantal relationship of intimacy, troth, and betrothal with the world. Christians are incurable world lovers—even when it hurts—because we follow one who so loved the world that he gave his only Son.

And so the apostle goes on to write, "let the peace of Christ rule in your hearts . . . be thankful . . . let the word of Christ dwell in you richly . . . teach one another in all wisdom . . . with gratitude . . . giving thanks" (3:15–16). Kind of interesting that he repeats the idea of gratitude three times in two verses.

---

3. Wright, *New Testament and the People of God*, 64; *History and Eschatology*, 205–14.

Actually, he'll bring it in one more time in the very next verse: "And whatever you do in word or deed, do everything in the name of our Lord Jesus Christ, giving thanks to God the Father through him" (3:17). Thinking Christianly is a matter of engaging the world in deep, deep gratitude. This is an epistemology of gratitude that refuses to take the world for granted, but instead always receives the world as a wonderful gift.

The word of Christ dwells in us, Paul writes. The word of Christ, the word of the gift of all gifts, takes up residence in our community, in our thoughts, in our hearts, in our day-to-day cultural endeavors. And when that word dwells in us, we teach in wisdom. We seek to see things whole, we strive for a knowing of the world that is directed towards integrality, healing, and communality. And we seek to know the world in a way that brings healing because we know the world through suffering eyes and bleeding hands. We know the world through the eyes of the Prince of Peace on a cross. We know the world and imagine the world from the perspective of shalom, and we seek the shalom of this world in defiance of its enmity, strife, and war.

What about worship?
Yes, what about worship?
Remember that the text places this teaching in wisdom, this growing in knowledge—maybe even this notion of thinking Christianly—in the context of worship: "and with gratitude in your hearts sing psalms, hymns, and spiritual songs to God" (3:16).
That's a good place to end. You see, one of the insights of so-called worldview thinking was that all of life is necessarily religious. We are, if you will, *homo religiosus*. Everything that we do—in word or deed, as Paul puts it in the next verse—is done in service, indeed in worship. The only question is, which god is worshipped in our words, our thinking, our imagining, our hoping, and our deeds?

Whether we are talking about choosing a stock portfolio or a spouse, writing poetry or urban planning, engaging in local politics or in the preservation of a watershed, having babies or starting a business—whatever we do is done as an act of worship.

The only question is, which god are we worshipping? From Paul's perspective, everything we do and everything we think is either rooted in the gospel narrative and committed to the gospel vision of authentic humanity or it's rooted and committed to an another story, another god.

I guess that thinking Christianly is a matter of placing all that we do before Christ as an act of worship.

Quite the calling.
Yes, quite the calling.

4

Education for Homelessness or Homemaking?
The Christian College in a Postmodern Culture

(Co-authored with Steven Bouma-Prediger)

> i wonder if I'll end up like bernie in his dream
> a displaced person in some foreign border town
> waiting for a train part hope part myth
> while the station changes hands[1]

Agricultural reformer Wes Jackson once observed that undergraduate education in America today tends to be little more than "education for upward mobility." Indeed, he suggests that this is the only "major" that modern institutions of higher education seem to offer. As a result, he argues that precious little attention "is paid to educating the young to return home, or go to some other place, and dig in."[2] Kentucky poet-farmer and essayist Wendell

---

1. Bruce Cockburn, "How I Spent My Fall Vacation," *Humans,* 1980.
2. Jackson, *Becoming Native,* 3.

Berry echoes Jackson when he laments that education today often dislocates people from their native place to such a degree that it has created "a powerful class of itinerant professional vandals" who are "now pillaging the country and laying it waste."[3] And environmental studies pioneer David Orr makes a similar claim with respect to American higher education when he states that "the conventional wisdom holds that all education is good, and the more of it one has, the better.... The truth is that without significant precautions, education can equip people merely to be more effective vandals of the earth."[4]

In our judgment, these perceptive cultural critics are right. Colleges and universities—small or large, public or private, Christian or secular—tend to educate for upward mobility, to alienate people from their local habitation, and to encourage the vandalization of the earth. In short, education today is in many respects education for global homelessness. In this chapter we explore these claims about contemporary education, in order to set forth an alternative vision of education and to describe some of the practical implications of such a biblically informed vision. Our thesis is simple: We propose that Christian higher education ought explicitly to aim at homecoming and homemaking.

This is an experimental essay. Our question is: What happens if we allow "homecoming" to be the guiding metaphor for our educational praxis? Erazim Kohak has wisely noted that metaphors "shape the context of our experience as a meaningful whole, deciding in the process not only what is primary and what derivative, but also who we ought to be and how we ought to act." In this sense, "a metaphor is a mask that molds the wearer's face."[5] And Neil Postman demonstrates specifically how metaphors shape the educational task.[6] So, if the real metaphor of higher education in America is that of "upward mobility," and if it is this metaphor that shapes our view of the student as client, customer, resource, professional-in-training, and

3. Berry, *Home Economics*, 50.
4. Orr, *Earth in Mind*, 5.
5. Kohak, "Of Dwelling," 31.
6. Postman, *End of Education*, esp. ch. 9.

citizen, then what happens if we shift the metaphor? What happens if we abandon upward mobility as the homeless-making metaphor that it is, secede from this education for homelessness, and choose instead to foster an education for homemaking? What would that look like? If biblical faith shapes an imagination in which this world is our creational home, then homelessness is the result of misplaced faith and failed stewardship; and, if the hope of redemption is for nothing less than the homecoming of God to a restored earth, then "homemaking" is a good candidate for a guiding metaphor in Christian educational endeavors.[7]

To try to unpack something of what this might look like we will first revisit Jackson, Berry, and Orr to understand better their complaint. Then we will follow the lead of Berry and Orr to provisionally and imaginatively suggest what such a homemaking vision might look like if it became formative of our educational practice.

EDUCATION FOR HOMELESSNESS

Wes Jackson

Wes Jackson contends that much of college and university education is education for upward mobility. Rather than learning how to become native to one's place—to know the people and plants and animals and customs of a particular locale and thus to live sustainably in that place—we are socialized into a materialistic way of life that blinds us to both the cultural and the ecological realities of our community and our landscape. We assume we will (and should) move upward—up the socio-economic ladder—and become more mobile, moving from place to place. And we assume that these are unalloyed goods—good by their very nature. We do not question that upward mobility might not be such a good thing. But such a socialization process, Jackson contends, leaves us ecologically illiterate.

---

7. On homemaking as an integrating metaphor for biblical faith see Bouma-Prediger and Walsh, *Beyond Homelessness*, esp. ch. 1 and all interludes; Volf and McAnnally-Linz, *Home of God*; and Brown and Tomlin, eds., *Coming Home*.

To test the plausibility of Jackson's claim, we need only ask ourselves a few questions. How many of our students know the trees that line the sidewalks on which they walk to and from class? How many of our students know the watershed from which their drinking water comes? How many of our students know where "away" is when they "throw things away"? If our students have no such specific knowledge of their peculiar place and how it works, how will they know how to take care of it, and why would they want to?

But "education for upward mobility" doesn't just result in ecological illiteracy. Students who have no intention of staying anywhere too long also demonstrate a profound geopolitical, historical, and aesthetic ignorance. Without any sense of commitment to place, one pays no attention to neighbors, cares little about the dynamics of local community politics, never comes to understand the stories that have shaped this place to be the place it is, and never hangs around long enough to appreciate the art, literature, poetry, and folk traditions that this place has fostered. One never becomes a homecomer or homemaker because one is lost in the homelessness of mobility. To borrow metaphors from Kohak, education for upward mobility is education for wayfaring nomads who know nothing of the virtues of dwelling, the importance of roots, and love for place.[8]

What if, Jackson muses, colleges and universities were to "assume the awesome responsibility to both validate and educate those who want to be homecomers—not necessarily to go home but to go somewhere and dig in and begin the long search and experiment to become native?"[9] What if, in order to achieve the sort of sustainable way of life that we must achieve in a shrinking world of limits, we worked toward "becoming native to our places in a coherent community that is in turn embedded in the ecological realities of its surrounding landscape"?[10] What if, given that upward mobility is often just a cipher for a kind of rootlessness

---

8. Kohak, "Of Dwelling," 36—42
9. Jackson, *Becoming Native*, 97.
10. Jackson, *Becoming Native*, 3.

and homelessness seemingly pervasive in our postmodern culture, institutions of higher education offered a "homecoming major"?[11]

Wendell Berry

Wendell Berry takes Wes Jackson's insights a step further. The "powerful class of itinerant professional vandals" that are pillaging our world and "laying it to waste" are the products (the metaphor is intentional) of an educational system that is governed by the superstition that the proper place in society of an educated person is "up." "Up is the direction from small to big," Berry comments. "Education is the way up. The popular aim of education is to put everybody 'on top.'" Berry then wryly comments, "Well, I think that I hardly need to document the consequent pushing and tramping and kicking in the face" in order to get on top and stay there.[12] We need to ask ourselves, and Berry will force us to ask ourselves, what are Christians doing "on top" of such a pile? What are Christians doing playing the same game of competitive upward mobility as everyone else? And why on earth are Christian educational institutions in this game? Perhaps we need to muse, with Berry, that "up" is "the wrong direction."[13]

Berry supports his claim about rampaging professionals with two observations. First, such folk must be "'upwardly mobile' transients who will permit no stay or place to interrupt their personal advance." They "must have no local allegiances" for "in order to be able to desecrate, endanger, or destroy a place . . . one must be able to leave it and forget it."[14] Success requires a transient mobility that

---

11. Jackson, *Becoming Native*, 3. On the rootlessness of postmodern life, see Wachtel, *Poverty of Affluence;* and Middleton and Walsh, *Truth is Stranger*, esp. ch. 7.

12. Berry, *What are People For?*, 25.

13. Berry, *What are People For?*, 26. Reflecting on the necessity of downward mobility later in the book, Berry writes, "We must achieve the character and acquire the skills to live much poorer than we do. We must waste less. We must work more for ourselves and each other" (201). We can just see it now—a new campaign by a leading Christian college: "the school of downward mobility"!

14. Berry, *Home Economics*, 51.

necessarily results in homelessness. The kind of careerism taken for granted in much of American culture implies that "one must never be able to think of any place as one's home; one must never think of any place as anyone else's home."[15] In such a context, successfully educated people "cannot take any place seriously because they must be ready at any moment, by the terms of power and wealth in the modern world, to destroy any place."[16] Placelessness and perpetual homelessness lie at the root of ecological vandalism.

Berry's second observation is that higher education is complicit in this vandalizing of the earth. As usual he minces no words:

> Many of these professionals have been educated, at considerable public expense, in colleges or universities that had originally a clear mandate to serve localities or regions—to receive the daughters and sons of their region, educate them, and send them home again to serve and strengthen their communities. The outcome shows, I think, that they have generally betrayed this mandate, having worked instead to uproot the best brains and talents, to direct them away from home into exploitative careers in one or another of the professions, and so to make them predators of communities and homelands, their own as well as other people's.[17]

Loyalty to profession supersedes loyalty to place and in that supersession everything is superseded. Berry is worth citing again at length:

> According to the new norm, the child's destiny is not to succeed the parents, but to outmode them; succession has given way to supersession. And this norm is

---

15. Berry, *Home Economics*, 51.

16. Wendell Berry, *Sex, Economy*, 22. On the connection between homelessness and ecological degradation see John F. Haught, "Religious and Cosmic Homelessness."

17. Berry, *Home Economics*, 51–52. Berry makes a similar point in *Gift of Good Land* in which he argues that schools are "powerful agents of the 'United States economy.' They do not prepare young people to stay at home and make the most of the best local opportunities. They serve the idea that it is good to produce little and consume much." (73)

institutionalized not in great communal stories, but in the education system. The schools are no longer oriented to a cultural inheritance that it is their duty to pass on unimpaired, but to the career, which is to say the future, of the child.... The child is not educated to return home and be of use to the place and community; he or she is educated to *leave* home and earn money in a provisional future that has nothing to do with place or community.[18]

Mobility replaces mindfulness. Homelessness banishes homecoming. Not only is going to college the first step "away from home," the educational endeavor itself propels one even farther from home, never to return.

An educational system established to train producers and consumers for a global market and rooted in an absolutization of efficiency and profitability is only successful when it produces docile and numb citizens who conform "to a rootless and placeless monoculture of commercial expectations and products."[19] It is not surprising, therefore, that the literature of "Generation X" is suffused with such images of placeless numbness. Writing in *Life After God*, Douglas Coupland confesses, "I have never really felt like I was 'from' anywhere; home to me ... is a shared electronic dream of cartoon memories, half-hour sitcoms and national tragedies." As such, Coupland says that he speaks with no distinct accent, or more accurately, he speaks with "the accent of nowhere—the accent of a person who has no fixed home in their mind."[20] Wendell Berry would say that the system has succeeded perfectly in producing such a generation of homeless young people. And it is no wonder, then that we have seen nothing less than the "unsettling of America."[21] The double meaning is quite intentional—the unsettling of America—its suburbanization,

---

18. Berry, *What are People For?*, 162–63. Perhaps a small correction is necessary here. It would be naive to suggest that any education, at any time, passed on a cultural inheritance "unimpaired." Teaching—like all of life—is an interpretive endeavor and therefore always "impairs" in one way or another.

19. Berry, *Sex, Economy*, 151.

20. Coupland, *Life After God*, 174.

21. Berry, *Unsettling of America*.

mallification, McDonaldification—is unsettling and disturbing to those who perceive what is being lost and why.[22]

Let us now turn from Wendell Berry to another prophet who rails against the homelessness of the modern consumer, David Orr.

David Orr

Here is Orr's telling question: If we are the most educated people in history, then why is the world under such profound ecological threat? Why are such highly educated people so ecologically blind, stupid, and malevolent? Why does a rise in linguistic literacy seem to parallel a concomitant increase in ecological illiteracy? Might it be that it is precisely *because* of our education that we are so ignorant of how the world works?[23]

Orr's thesis is devastatingly simple. "Education," he says, "is no guarantee of decency, prudence, or wisdom. More of the same kind of education will only compound our problems."[24] Indeed, Orr insists that our current patterns of education will only foster more ecological illiteracy precisely because such educational practices are rooted in a series of debilitating falsehoods that all conspire to render us displaced persons. For example, the belief that the earth can be satisfactorily managed with enough scientific and technological know-how, and that where there is an increase in the accumulation of information there is a concomitant increase

---

22. See also William Leach, *Country of Exiles*; and James Kunstler, *Geography of Nowhere*, and its sequel, *Home from Nowhere*.

23. Sadly, this is not a new question or a new suspicion about "modern" education. Pioneering environmentalist Aldo Leopold perceptively raised the same problems fifty years ago: "One of the requisites of an ecological comprehension of land is an understanding of ecology, and this is by no means coextensive with 'education'; in fact, much higher education seems deliberately to avoid ecological concepts." *Sand County Almanac*, 262.

24. Orr, *Earth in Mind*, 8. Orr's argument bears some resemblance to Jonathan Kozol's meditation on education in the 1970s, *Night is Dark*, in which he asked how it could be that American boys in Vietnam could have committed the atrocities at My Lai. What went wrong in the American education system so that these all-American boys could have become such monsters? Kozol's conclusion: nothing went wrong at all. The system works perfectly.

in wisdom and knowledge, is foundational to the modern educational enterprise. Moreover, says Orr, higher education in the West is also directed by the technicistic belief that we can restore what we have dismantled. And all of this happens within the context of an arrogant metanarrative of cultural superiority that is the mythological foundation of the whole educational/cultural enterprise.[25] Such education, so the myth goes, will make us better people.[26]

Now Orr's problem with such an approach to education isn't simply its unabashed arrogance and hubris. Rather, like Jackson and Berry, he sees the devastating effect of this kind of education in socio-ecological life. An information-driven education that is directed to scientific and technological control of a world that is here for our dismantling and restoration, all fuelled by an economic imperative that is identified with the very direction of civilization and the moral progress of humanity, spells disaster for our relation to ecosystems broadly speaking and local places in particular.

In the end, Orr says, such an educational practice produces people who relate to their world as "residents" rather than "inhabitants." And a culture of residents is a culture of homelessness. In his *Ecological Literacy*, Orr explains this distinction at some length. "The resident is a temporary and rootless occupant who mostly needs to know where the banks and stores are in order to plug in." By contrast, the inhabitant cannot be separated from a particular habitat "without doing violence to both . . ." "To reside is to live as a transient and as a stranger to one's place, and inevitably to some part of the self." The inhabitant and place, however, "mutually shape each other."[27]

Later he expands on this distinction:

25. Compare this with Bob Goudzwaard's classic discussion of the progress motif in Western culture, *Capitalism and Progress*.

26. Echoing similar sentiments, Wendell Berry says that one of the foundational assumptions of "commercial education" (by which he means pretty much all formal education in America) is that, "educated people are better than other people because education improves people and makes them good." *Sex, Economy*, xiii.

27. Orr, *Ecological Literacy*, 102.

A resident is a temporary occupant, putting down few roots and investing little, knowing little, and perhaps caring little for the immediate locale beyond its ability to gratify.... The inhabitant, by contrast, "dwells," as [Ivan] Illich puts it, in an intimate, organic, and mutually nurturing relationship with a place. Good inhabitance is an art requiring detailed knowledge of a place, the capacity for observation, and a sense of care and rootedness.[28]

And so while residents require only "cash and a map," inhabitants "bear the marks of their places," and when uprooted get homesick. And this is so because for the inhabitant, there is a place of dwelling in which one finds identity and from which one derives meaning and apart from which one feels lost and lonely. In short, "the plain fact is that the planet does not need more successful people," more residents; rather, "it needs more people who live well in their places," more inhabitants.[29]

Postmodern Homelessness

Jackson, Berry, and Orr would all agree that contemporary education at all stages, but most decidedly at the university level, is a process of forming people who will be residents, not inhabitants. This is an education of upward mobility that results in a pedagogy of disconnection and an ethos of displacement. In the context of a global economy, higher education produces career-oriented consumers who have no intimate knowledge of, or sense of commitment to, any place. This is an education for homelessness.

It is no surprise then, that the postmodern condition is so often described in terms of homelessness.[30] Postmodern a/theologian Mark Taylor describes the postmodern self as a "wanderer," a

---

28. Orr, *Ecological Literacy*, 130. The reference to Illich is to his essay, "Dwelling."

29. Orr, *Earth in Mind*, 12.

30. We have addressed themes of postmodern homelessness at greater length in Walsh, "Homemaking in Exile," Bouma-Prediger, "Yearning for Home," and together in *Beyond Homelessness*, ch. 7.

"drifter," "attached to no home," and "always suspicious of stopping, staying and dwelling."³¹ Interestingly, such a postmodern homeless drifter bears more than a casual resemblance to the endlessly acquisitive ego of late modernity, consuming the products, and more importantly, the images, that global capitalism serves up.³² The commodification of all of life, most fully realized in the imperial regime of global capitalism, renders us all restless and insatiable consumers, unable to settle, permanently exiled from home.³³ Elie Wiesel is right. Ours is the age of the expatriate, the refugee, and the wanderer. "Never before have so many fled from so many homes."³⁴ But this is no longer exclusively the socio-cultural condition of the politically, ethnically, and economically oppressed. We are now all in exile, all displaced, all disconnected from any sense of place that could carry the full weight of the notion of home. And education has been a co-conspirator in producing this culture of homelessness.

EDUCATION FOR HOMEMAKING

Wendell Berry, again

Commenting on Wallace Stegner's contrast between "boomers" and "stickers"—which roughly parallel's Orr's residents and inhabitants, or Kohak's wayfarers and dwellers—Wendell Berry writes, that "if enough of us were to choose caring over not caring, staying over going, then the culture would change, the theme of exploitation would become subordinate to the theme of settlement, and

---

31. Taylor, *Erring*, 150, 157, 156, 147. Following Richard Bernstein, it is fair to say that Jacques Derrida's deconstructive project is "always encouraging us to question the status of what we take to be our center, our native home, our arche." *New Constellation*, 183.

32. We echo here Roger Lundin, who has suggested that, "The desiring and acquiring self of postmodern cultural theory bears more than a casual resemblance to the unit of consumption at the center of market economies and democratic societies." *Culture of Interpretation*, 73–74.

33. On the connection between postmodernity and global capitalism see Boyle, *Who Are We Now?*, and Hauerwas, "Christian Difference."

34. Wiesel, "Longing for Home," 19.

then the choice to be a sticker would become easier."[35] Herein is Berry's hope and program—to encourage stickers, dwellers and inhabitants who have a love of place. But, while "commercial education"[36] sees the school, especially the college and university, as an "economic resource"[37] in a competition for wealth and power, Berry calls for an education that is accountable to what he calls the "party of local community."[38]

The party of the local community believes that "the neighborhood, the local community, is the proper place and frame of reference for responsible work."[39] Therefore, an education that would recognize that locality is the proper scale of human endeavor—of human stewardship—would be an education that helps students "acquire a competent knowledge of local geography, ecology, history, natural history and local songs and stories."[40] According to Berry, such an emphasis on locality is neither a matter of a romantic return to roots, nor merely an escape from the anonymity of urban life. Rather, the focus on locality is a matter of societal, ecological, and cultural preservation and sustainability. It is a matter of ending the ecological and economic vandalism of the highly educated professional class in a global culture of homelessness and fostering an alternative vision of homecoming. But such homecoming is impossible without a love, care, knowledge, and intimacy with place.

In an address at a conference some years ago, Richard Mouw cited Craig Dykstra's conviction that scholarship and education that is decidedly Christian must be a scholarship and education that "sees deeply into the reality of things and loves that reality."[41] Berry would profoundly concur. But he would add that such love and such seeing is never generic, it is never universal, it is always

---

35. Berry, *Another Turn*, 70.
36. Berry, *Sex, Economy*, xii—xiv.
37. Berry, *What are People For?*, 133
38. Berry, *Another Turn*, 17.
39. Berry, *Another Turn*, 17.
40. Berry, *Another Turn*, 40.
41. Mouw, "Assessing Christian Scholarship."

placed, timed, and particular. Just as we cannot love our neighbor "in general," but must always love *this* neighbor, here in *this* neighborhood, so also can we never love things in general or the world in general, or even creation in general, apart from a love, intimacy, knowledge, and care for a particular place. Indeed, Berry insists that the love of learning cannot exist apart from the love of place and community. "Without this love, education is only the importation into the local community of centrally prescribed 'career preparation' designed to facilitate the export of young careerists."[42] And then we are back to homelessness all over again. If you love your community, Berry says, you must oppose such education with all of your might. So we need to ask not only the abstract question, "Christian education—for what?," but the more concrete and personal questions, "Christian education—for whom?" and "for where?"

Christian scholarship and education, we are arguing, must be for the shaping and formation of Christian community. This is, we acknowledge, a variation on themes that have been developed by people like Nicholas Wolterstorff, Thomas Groome, Craig Dykstra, and Parker Palmer.[43] But the Berryian twist on these themes of character and community is to note that "if the word *community* is to mean or to amount to anything, it must refer to a place (in its natural integrity) and its people. It must refer to a placed people." And concurrently, "persons of character are not public products" of mass education. Rather, "they are made by local cultures, local responsibilities."[44]

In the face of a culture of disconnected homelessness, however, such locality—such placedness—requires the fostering of a connected intimacy that runs counter to the abstract distance that characterizes modern education and technological society. Even terms like "ecology" and "ecosystems," says Berry, "come from the juiceless abstract intellectuality of the universities that was

42. Berry, *What are People For?*, 164.
43. Wolterstorff, *Educating for Responsible Action;* Groome, *Sharing Faith;* Dykstra, *Vision and Character;* Palmer, *To Know as We are Known.*
44. Berry, *What are People For?*, 26.

invented to disconnect, displace, and disembody the mind." An education for homemaking, however, would insist that "the real names of the environment are the names of rivers and river valleys; creeks, ridges, and mountains; towns and cities; lakes, woodlands, lanes, roads, creatures, and people."[45]

According to Berry, there are at least two things that are required if we are to shift the paradigm of education from homelessness to homemaking, from vandalism to care. The first is that our education must engender an ethos of intimacy and affection.[46] This would require, we think, an abandonment of both the aggressive realism of modernist epistemology and the equally anthropocentric (and usually equally aggressive) anti-realist constructivism of postmodernism. In its place we would propose a relational epistemology rooted in a relational ontology. And since we confess that this relationship is rooted in God's extravagant creational love, knowing this world is always, at heart, a matter of love. N. T. Wright describes such an epistemology of love beautifully when he says, "The lover affirms the reality and the otherness of the beloved. Love does not seek to collapse the beloved in terms of itself." In such an epistemology, "'love' will mean 'attention': the readiness to let the other *be* the other, the willingness to grow and change in oneself in relation to the other."[47] Educational theorist Parker Palmer makes a similar point when he says that "the act of knowing *is* an act of love, the act of entering and embracing the reality of the other, of allowing the other to enter and embrace our own."[48] We suspect that Berry would agree.

But there is a second thing that Berry says is required if we are to reaffirm community and place in all of our praxis, not least in education. And that is that in the name of community, for the love of place, and, most profoundly, for the sake of Christian discipleship, we must secede from the empire that has rendered us

---

45. Berry, *Sex, Economy*, 35.

46. Berry, *Sex, Economy*, 168.

47. Wright, *New Testament and the People of God*, 64. Such an epistemology is explored further in Keesmaat and Walsh, *Colossians Remixed*, ch. 7.

48. Palmer, *To Know*, 8.

homeless. We know that this is a rather sensitive time to be talking about empire, but if the forces of displacement, disconnectedness, and homelessness are imperially imposed, then we must speak of empire. And Berry does not mince his words about Christianity and empire:

> Despite its protests to the contrary, modern Christianity has become willy-nilly the religion of the state and the economic status quo.... It has, for the most part, stood silently by while a predatory economy has ravaged the world, destroyed its natural beauty and health, divided and plundered its communities and households. It has flown the flag and chanted the slogans of empire. It has assumed with the economists that "economic forces" automatically work for good and has assumed with the industrialists and militarists that technology determines history. It has assumed with almost everybody that "progress" is good, that it is good to be modern and up with the times. It has admired Caesar and comforted him in his degradations and faults. But in its de facto alliance with Caesar, Christianity connives directly in the murder of Creation.[49]

The degree to which this prophetic critique of the modern church is true is the degree to which it is also true of Christian higher education and scholarship. In response to this, Berry advocates "a quiet secession by which people find the practical means and the strength of spirit to remove themselves from the economy that is exploiting them and destroying their homeland."[50] In his poem, "The Mad Farmer, Flying the Flag of Rough Branch, Secedes from the Union," Berry calls us to secede from the union of power and money, government and science, science and money, genius and war, and "from outer space and inner vacuity."[51] An education for homemaking joins in such a secessionist movement.[52]

49. Berry, *Sex, Economy*, 114–15.
50. Berry, *Sex, Economy*, 17–18.
51. Berry, *Selected Poems*, 162–63.
52. Berry's secessionism bears some resonance with Hauerwas and Willimon, *Resident Aliens*.

David Orr is a member of this movement. Let us now consider his contribution to an education for homemaking.

David Orr, again

An education for homemaking is rooted in the belief that this earth is truly our home. This planet, created good by God and one day to be renovated by that same promise-keeping God, is our home. To be faithful homemakers, therefore, we must know something about our home planet. This implies that we must educate for increased ecological literacy. Just as we educate for numeracy, or the ability to calculate, and literacy, or the ability to read, so also we must educate for understanding how the world works. At the risk of running into Berry's critique of juiceless intellectualism, let's call this an education in "ecolacy."[53]

But what exactly is ecolacy? What does it mean to be ecologically literate? David Orr describes the essence of ecological literacy as "that quality of mind that seeks out connections."[54] In contrast to the narrow specialization that characterizes so much education today, an ecological frame of mind seeks to integrate, to bring together, to see things whole. "The ecologically literate person has the knowledge necessary to comprehend interrelatedness, and an attitude of care or stewardship," and this must be accompanied by "the practical competence required to act on the basis of knowledge and feeling." Hence "knowing, caring, and practical competence constitute the heart of ecological literacy."[55] We must not only know, we must care. And we must not only care, we must have the wherewithal to act responsibly.

But concretely what does this mean? Orr offers a list of five necessary components of seeing things whole. First, we need "a broad understanding of how people and societies relate to each other and to natural systems, and how they might do so

---

53. Garrett Hardin seems to have coined the term in *Filters Against Folly*, 24. And see all of his ch. 7.

54. Orr, *Ecological Literacy*, 92.

55. Orr, *Ecological Literacy*, 92.

sustainably."[56] This presumes knowledge of how the world as a physical system works—knowledge of keystone species and succession, entropy and energy flow, niches and food chains. Ecological literacy, in short, implies a modicum of knowledge about the interconnectedness of all creatures great and small. In biblical terms, this is wisdom.

Second, we need to know "something of the speed of the crisis that is upon us."[57] Hence, we need to know the vital signs of our home planet—the trends concerning population growth and climate change, soil loss and species extinction, deforestation and desertification, energy use and air pollution. A prescription is only as good as the diagnosis on which it is based. Our attempts to achieve wellness must, therefore, be based on a sober assessment of the health of the earth. Biblically, this is the ability to read the signs of the times, the ability to have prophetic discernment.

Third, ecological literacy, according to Orr, "requires a comprehension of the dynamics of the modern world."[58] In other words, we need some understanding of the historical, political, economic, and religious forces that have molded the contemporary world. What ideas and social pressures have brought us to where we are today? Ecological literacy, then, requires a well-rounded interdisciplinary education.

Fourth, ecological literacy requires "broad familiarity with the development of ecological consciousness."[59] Of special importance here is explicit attention to ethics and the nature of nature. Are we humans, for example, "conqueror of the land-community" or "plain member and citizen of it"?[60] Is the natural world "red in tooth and claw" or some Edenic paradise of harmony? Or perhaps neither but something else? Such an issue is of great importance, for whether and how we "follow nature," depends in large part on

---

56. Orr, *Ecological Literacy*, 92.
57. Orr, *Ecological Literacy*, 93.
58. Orr, *Ecological Literacy*, 93.
59. Orr, *Ecological Literacy*, 94.
60. Leopold, *Sand County*, 240. See also Wirzba, *From Nature to Creation*.

our idea of what nature is and of who we are as humans.[61] If we are to be homecomers and to love and care for a place, then we need to know what our "place" is. Biblically speaking, this is the doctrine of creation.

Fifth and finally, Orr maintains that we need "alternative measures of well-being" and "a different approach to technology." For example, Herman Daly and John Cobb's "Index of Sustainable Economic Welfare," in contrast to other indicators such as "Gross Domestic Product," includes the depletion of nonrenewable natural resources and the costs of water and air pollution in its calculation of overall welfare.[62] And the work of E. F. Schumacher, to mention only one well-known example, illustrates how technology can and must be appropriate to the scale and needs of a people and its culture.[63] Again, biblically this is a matter of wisdom.

Echoing one of the central tenets of the Christian tradition, Orr says that ecological literacy is "built on a view of ourselves as finite and fallible creatures living in a world limited by natural laws."[64] Ecological literacy, in other words, is founded upon the theological insight that we are creatures—limited and liable to error—living in a world not of our own making. Being ecologically literate is, simply, knowing the rules of the house, and knowing those rules ought to engender a humble and thoughtful keeping of this God's blue-green earth.[65]

So what is an education for homemaking? It is at the very least, an education directed to ecolacy, directed to precisely that kind of intimacy and knowledge of place that Wendell Berry has been calling for. But of course this is, in itself, not enough. An education for homemaking requires much more.

---

61. Rolston III, *Environmental Ethics*, 32.
62. Daly and Cobb Jr., *Common Good*, 401–56.
63. Schumacher, *Small is Beautiful*.
64. Orr, *Ecological Literacy*, 95.
65. Bouma-Prediger develops these themes further in *Creation Care*, and *Earthkeeping and Character*.

HOMEMAKING, HOMELESSNESS, AND HOSPITALITY

Earlier in this chapter we talked briefly about the significance of metaphors for shaping educational praxis. And we have asked what an education that is shaped by the guiding metaphor of homemaking might be. A closely related metaphor to home is that of hospitality. Home without hospitality is more akin to a fortress of exclusion and self-protection than anything that would cut through our disconnected placelessness with a place-shaped community. In a post-September 11, 2001 world, the last thing we need is that kind of stance in defense of the "homeland." Down that path there is only more homelessness. Rather, home in the face of the other—especially the homeless or oppressed other—can never be a fortress. On this point, Emmanuel Levinas taps deeper springs of biblical insight with his insistence on the priority of the other who "paralyzes possession" of the home in order to keep home open to hospitality.[66]

David I. Smith and Barbara Carvill have suggested that hospitality to the stranger can serve as a "metaphor for the way both teachers and students understand and interact with otherness."[67] And while their discussion of the implications of such a metaphor clearly bears fruit in the area of foreign language education, education as hospitality is also thoroughly congruent with the direction of our proposal for education as homemaking. Hospitality, within the ethos of the classroom, in response to legitimate plurality and as an epistemological stance vis-à-vis the world is, we think, deeply homemaking.

And, of course, there would be something profoundly perverse about a discussion of an education for homemaking without addressing the pressing problems of geopolitical and economic homelessness. If it is tragically ironic that an increase in literacy seems to always accompany an increase in ecological illiteracy, then it is doubly tragic that a culture of affluent, upwardly mobile

---

66. Levinas, *Totality and Infinity*, 171.
67. Smith and Carvill, *Gift*, 88.

nomads should also produce millions of people who have literally no roof over their heads. This is truly a culture of homelessness, and the people on our inner-city streets, together with the international refugees lined up at our borders seeking economic, political and ethnic refuge bear witness to the moral bankruptcy of our culture and the complicity of education in that bankruptcy. Precisely because an education for homemaking is an education rooted in hospitality, Christian scholarship is called to shape character, communities, economic and political structures, and churches in such a way that they offer a place for the placeless and a home for the homeless.

So Christian higher education—for whom? For the homeless in our midst. The homeless wanderers that we have all become. For the homemaking God who is coming. And Christian higher education—for where? For our neighborhoods, our streams, our forests. For God's good earth. And Christian higher education—for what? For homemaking in the kingdom of God. For the restoration of the creational home.[68] For repairing the breach and restoring streets to live in.[69]

---

68. For a vigorous critique of this article see Klay and Lunn, "Reflection," and our response, Bouma-Prediger and Walsh, "Response."

69. Isa 58:12.

5

Meredith on the Subway
A Story of Displacement and Homemaking

MEREDITH ON THE SUBWAY

The platform is crowded with people getting increasingly late for work because the subway trains aren't moving. It is Bathurst Station in Toronto and there seems to be a security issue of some sort. The whole system has shut down until things can be cleared in the very station where Meredith is waiting to get on a train for work. What's going on? Did someone jump? Maybe a bomb threat? Has a crime been committed? Should she be worried about her safety?

No fewer than ten police officers arrive and the problem becomes clear. They surround a teenage boy sitting on the platform. They cuff him and begin interrogating him. The train doors open and everyone squeezes on board—everyone except Meredith. The boy is Black. He doesn't seem to understand why he has attracted so much attention from the Toronto Police Services. He is surrounded by large officers. Meredith isn't leaving.

She goes over to the scene and stands there. She doesn't aggressively question what the police are doing to this young man. She doesn't pull out her cellphone to record what is going on. She just stands there. When asked to give the officers some space, she politely takes two steps back. But only two steps. She isn't leaving. Her motive is clear and simple: this young Black boy is surrounded by police officers because somehow he is perceived as a security threat. And Meredith figures that in the sea of faces around this boy, there needs to be at least one face that is supportive, one face expressing care, one face that is there *for* him, not against him. She remains nearby to bear witness, to claim her space, and to take a stand (physically and figuratively). She determines that it is her "place" to stand in solidarity with this young man whose "place" on the subway system is literally threatened with dis-place-ment into police custody.

You see, someone saw a Swiss Army knife fall out of this boy's pocket while he was resting on the platform. That knife occasioned an emergency call to the police, which resulted in significant delays for the whole subway system that morning. But the boy's crime wasn't really the knife. It was the color of his skin. Meredith knew that if a fine-looking, well-dressed white boy had a little pocketknife like that fall out of his pocket, there would be no emergency call to police because there would have been no perceived threat. But Black kids get different treatment.

This story reminds me of two of my teenage Sunday school students some years ago. Mathew and Matthias were both studying violin, and they were both often late for their lessons. So, it wouldn't be a surprise to see either of them running down the street with a violin case in hand. But only Mathew was ever stopped by the police—and more than once! Only Mathew, a Black kid, ever seemed suspicious to the police as he ran to his lesson with a violin case in hand. To the police, seeing Mathew run with his case meant something was out of place, something wasn't fitting with the picture of society, something just wasn't right. Yet, when Matthias, a white boy, did the same thing, nothing was out of place at all.

So, in a similar situation of racial and cultural displacement, Meredith stood there on the subway platform to bear witness; she only left when it was clear that the lad was not going to be arrested and only after she had caught his eye to make sure that he was okay. Late for work, she told the story to her boss, who thanked her for doing what she did. You see, Meredith noticed this boy in a precarious place—indeed, in a place where it was deemed he had *no* place—and determined that it was her "place" to stand there, bearing witness and being a living presence of support for this young neighbor.

And this was not the first time twenty-three-year-old Meredith had intervened on the subway. Let me tell you another Meredith story.

As soon as the man stepped onto the subway car you could sense that there was going to be trouble. He took one look at the Muslim family nearby, a dad and mom with their young child, and began berating them. Standing over them, he launched into a threatening tirade of Islamophobic hatred, making it clear that to him these folks had no "place" on that subway, no place in this city, and no place in this country. But before he had two sentences out of his mouth, Meredith was out of her seat and had placed her imposing five-foot-four body between the man and the family. This behavior would not happen on her watch, in her presence, or on this subway car in her city. This man would not be allowed to intimidate this poor family without opposition. This family would not be left unprotected in the face of such violent racism. Before long, another man joined Meredith in defense of the family and gently ejected the offender from the train. Meredith stayed by the family's side until it was clear they felt safe. For this family, and for all of us, being safe and knowing that you belong are at the heart of having a sense of place, a sense of belonging, a sense of being at home.

There is an interesting twist to this story. The man berating the family bore all the marks of mental illness and perhaps homelessness. He himself suffered from displacement in our society. But, in order to defend the legitimate place of the family on the subway, this man had to be displaced yet again as he was evicted from that subway car. And who knows, maybe he was among the hundreds of unhoused people in Toronto who lived in the tent encampments around the city during the coronavirus pandemic. Maybe he was living in a tent at Trinity-Bellwoods Park on June 21, 2021 when a heavily militarized force aggressively and violently dismantled that encampment. But here's the thing: if he was there, so was Meredith. You see, this was yet another example of forced displacement against our most vulnerable neighbors, and once again, this would not go unopposed. Not on Meredith's watch. And so, Meredith and her sibling joined hundreds of others standing in solidarity at Trinity-Bellwoods Park, insisting that, all of the ambiguities of encampments notwithstanding, further displacing a community already deeply displaced was an act of violent injustice. And so Meredith was there, washing the pepper spray out of another protestor's eyes while her own eyes were full of tears of sorrow and rage.

From these stories, you might be getting the picture that Meredith makes a habit of this kind of thing. The truth is that she finds herself in such situations with some regularity. In his Narnia book *The Magician's Nephew*, C. S. Lewis wrote, "What you see and hear depends a good deal on where you are standing. It also depends on what sort of person you are."[1] Meredith found herself standing with a Black kid in trouble with the police, or a Muslim family threatened on the subway, or a community of unhoused folks who have gathered into an encampment community, because she was open to seeing the injustice and racism around her. She saw fear in the eyes of these neighbors. While others either saw a threat or simply averted their gaze, intentionally deciding to see nothing at all, Meredith saw these people as neighbors and so was compelled to act as a neighbor to them. You see, that's the "sort of person" that Meredith is. By making a habit of this kind of engagement with the world in everyday practices, by being neighborly even if it puts herself at some risk, Meredith both demonstrates her character

---

1. Lewis, *Magician's Nephew*, 125.

and continues to form the kinds of virtues that dispose her to inhabit the world in a certain way.

From racism to Islamophobia, homophobia, and transphobia; from the crisis of homelessness to ecological desecration; from refugees and forced migrations to the devastating and violent displacement and genocide in Palestine that we have borne witness to, we live in an age of displacement. And such displacement is always violent, always rooted in fear, and always dripping in resentment.

A Black boy on the subway platform can never forget that he is a Black boy. He can never get past the fear that his very presence creates in a society of white privilege. He may be a fourth-generation Canadian who is deeply rooted in this country, and maybe even this city, but the color of his skin and the discriminatory treatment he gets from the police are a constant reminder that he doesn't really belong. While a citizen, born and raised in this country, he is, nonetheless, displaced. Even if he is a hockey-playing, straight-A student who has never been in any trouble, he doesn't have the same "place" on that subway platform as a white kid does.

What about that Muslim family? Perhaps they are recent refugees from Syria, displaced by war, desperately trying to make a new home in a foreign land. But whether they are refugees or not, their skin color and the hijab worn by the mother clearly identify them as Muslim, and that means that they are marked out as a threat.

And what "place" do homeless folks have in taking over parks and other public spaces? Literally displaced through their houselessness, economically displaced by their poverty, socially displaced because of mental health or addiction struggles, and culturally displaced because they are an embarrassment to an upwardly mobile and affluent society, these neighbors find themselves violently displaced when they create their own semblance of neighborhood and community in a tent encampment. That so many of our unhoused neighbors are Indigenous, displaced from the land, their language, and their families in a history of genocide, only serves to remind us that displacement is at the very core of our colonial settler history.

Knowing this, Meredith cannot sit idly by. Of course, Meredith also knows something about displacement by virtue of her gender. She knows something of the kind of violent threat that these neighbors experience in daily life. But at the same time she has a deep experience of being placed, of being at home in the world. Maybe it was the way her family home was the gathering spot for all the kids on their street, regardless of race, ethnicity, or religion, that gave her this sense of place. Maybe it was all the people who came in and out of her family home, some staying for months, some just dropping in for dinner. For Meredith, home is a place of welcome and hospitality, a place to be extended to and shared with others.

Or maybe it was her work in theater, improv, and circus that attuned her to knowing where she was at any given time, and that gave her an awareness of what was going on around her. Maybe it was knowing folks in her life who were literally homeless on the streets of Toronto that attuned her to forced displacement.

Throughout her life Meredith has had deep friendships with people with intellectual disabilities, and maybe that has helped shape her as someone who will protect the vulnerable. Maybe her sense of justice and dignity was deepened through experiences in Central America, or by her trip to Palestine when she was a teenager. If anyone is displaced by means of oppressive and violent expropriation, surely it is the Palestinians. All of these experiences have formed Meredith in a way that has profoundly shaped her character and given her the kind of life orientation and disposition that is born of knowing one's place and knowing one's home.

DISPLACEMENT AND PLACELESSNESS

There is a difference between displacement and placelessness. The displaced are those who are, by various means, stripped of their place. Displacement is something that is imposed on people. Placelessness, however, is a cultural consequence of what James

Howard Kunstler calls a "geography of nowhere."[2] You see, whether we are talking about the upwardly mobile who view each place as a rung on the ladder that goes up to who-knows-where, or the postmodern nomad with no roots in any place or any tradition of place, or the average consumer who doesn't know anything about the place where they live or the places their food comes from, the reality is the same—we are a culture of placelessness. And while the displaced long for place, those who embrace placelessness just don't care. Indeed, those who embrace placelessness escape the requirements of place.[3] In the name of an undefined freedom, they embody a certain detachment in their lives, devoid of any commitment. Meredith, however, does not seek escape from difficult and even violent situations around her. Far from detachment, she deliberately attaches herself to threatened neighbors, demonstrating her commitment to them and to a freedom defined by justice. Meredith's experience of place brings responsibility for those who are displaced.

Folks who affirm placedness, and who insist on creating place for those who have been displaced, know that radical hospitality is at the heart of it all. There is no authentic experience of a place as home apart from hospitality, and a life devoid of hospitality is a life hell-bent on home-breaking. That's what was going on in both of the two subway confrontations and the homeless encampment. All three of these stories are about telling people that they have no legitimate "home" in our society. Meredith will not abide such home-breaking. If this city is home for her, then it must be home for all. And so her courageous interventions were about confronting home-breaking discrimination with homemaking hospitality.

PLACE, CHARACTER, AND VIRTUE

There can be no doubting Meredith's courage in these subway encounters, nor her passion. Meredith, like everyone who showed

---

2. Kunstler, *Geography of Nowhere*.
3. See Brueggemann, *Land*, ch. 1.

up to support their neighbors in tent encampments, lives in hope of a better world, a world of justice and compassion, of inclusion and equality. And while she has had to persevere, and continues to show remarkable resilience in the face of all kinds of struggles in her life, it is also evident that her passion and courage are rooted in a clear sense of vocation and calling. To not come to the aid of these subway neighbors would have been a betrayal of who she is called to be.

Meredith displays some of the key virtues, or character traits, of homemaking, and these virtues are all rooted in and deeply shaped by her sense of place, or emplacedness.[4] Her character has been formed in the particularity and stability of her family home, and in her family's commitment to local community-building through their political activism, food production, support of local products, community gardens, public institutions like the local libraries and parks, hospitable neighborliness, and ecological care. And, not surprisingly, she finds herself attracted to folks who manifest a similar character, folks who are also committed to place in a culture of displacement.

So far I have only told stories of protecting the sense of place for our displaced human neighbors. But the crisis of displacement in our time is not limited to these, admittedly tragic, tales of displaced people. Not only is displacement experienced as a loss of connection with a land in which we have a place—land that has formed our identity and our sense of geographical familiarity—but the current ecological crisis is itself a destruction of place, a murder of habitat for habitation. And any sense of place-making and place-defending in human relations can only have depth, creativity, and resilience if it is rooted in a deep ecological love of particular places, biospheres, watersheds, and geographies.

It is, therefore, not surprising that throughout her life Meredith has cared for animals small (kittens) and large (horses). She has spent time in the wilderness, at a summer camp committed

---

4. Bouma-Prediger and I address the shape of homemaking virtues at some length in *Beyond Homelessness*, ch. 6. See also Bouma-Prediger, *Earthkeeping and Character*.

to shaping ecological virtues in its campers, working in the family garden, and playing imaginative games with her friends in the forest. Nature does, indeed, nurture, and the longer one spends lovingly attentive to non-human creatures, the deeper one's sense of gratitude and contentment will be. Creation teaches compassion, care, and love because creation is born of the compassion, care, and love of the Creator.

What you see depends on where you stand and what sort of person you are, meaning what kind of character you inhabit. And character is shaped by the stories of our lives. Jamie Smith notes, "We live *into* the stories we've absorbed; we become characters in the drama that has captivated us. Thus much of our action is acting out a kind of script that has unconsciously captured our imaginations."[5] Our character is rooted in the stories of our lives. Those experiences in the subway have now become part of Meredith's narrative. And, as we have seen, those subway interventions are themselves rooted in the stories of place, family, oppression, vulnerability, joyous activism, engagement with nature, work, and friendship that have shaped Meredith to be the kind of person that she is. And there are, of course, also the stories that have shaped her imagination over the course of her young life. From the stories she was read at bedtime as a child, Meredith has been immersed in narratives of good and evil, of virtue and vice. In these stories she has seen how character is formed in the midst of deep struggle and conflict. Tales of creative and resilient resistance to injustice have been deeply formative for her.

But there is a larger story that is at the heart of Meredith's life—a grand story that has profoundly shaped her character. This story has sunk into her bones, provided a picture of what life is all about, and has captivated her imagination. We could almost say that she drank in this story with her mother's milk. This story has provided the primary drama in which Meredith is an actor. You see, Meredith was raised in a Christian home in which the stories of the Hebrew and Christian Scriptures, together with the liturgies of the church, were foundational. Of course, Christians have no

---

5. Smith, *Imagining the Kingdom*, 32.

monopoly on justice, and they have often not demonstrated a profound commitment to place, except perhaps their sacred spaces called churches. Nor does it appear to be necessary to be embedded in the biblical story to be a person or a community that embodies the virtues of place-making and place-defending. Nonetheless, the Bible is the foundational story that has shaped Meredith.

In this story Meredith learned that life is rooted in love and justice is required in the face of oppression. In this narrative it is the poor, those who mourn and who have nothing, who are blessed. This is an upside-down narrative in which the first become last and the last become first, and in which the displaced are given privilege of place in the coming reign of God. While so much of her culture shouts that it is the powerful and deceitful who are successful in the world, this alternative narrative teaches that it is the meek and the pure in heart who inherit the earth. Here Meredith learned the radical call to be merciful; here she learned that the deepest hunger is the hunger for justice. And it is here she learned that if you live an alternative life, seeking justice and defending the vulnerable, then that just might be dangerous. But since this story is about Jesus, crucified by the imperial powers in collusion with the religious establishment of the day, it is clear that danger, suffering, and sacrifice are at the heart of a life of love. Jesus creates a place for all, indeed a place for a new creation, through the radical displacement of the cross.

That, I think, is really at the heart of it. "Jesus creates a place for all, indeed a place for a new creation, through the radical displacement of the cross." Without the radical hope of a new creation, without a compelling vision of homecoming in the face of homelessness, of the renewal of places of shalom in the face of violent displacement, we will not have the spiritual or imaginative resources to confront the forces of displacement that wreak such suffering and destruction in our world.

Or perhaps we could say that Meredith has been driven by a vision of a new heavens and a new earth. Perhaps this is the vision found in Isaiah: a city—Jerusalem no less, which has been a site of such violence and displacement throughout its history—is now transformed into a place of welcome, delight, and joy. In this vision the healing of our displacement isn't through a further displacement out of our earthly home into some kind of placeless heaven. No, in this vision we find our hope in a grounded and restored placement in the earth from which we were born. This is a radical urban renewal in which

> weeping and sorrow will be no more—because no one will be excluded, no one will be violently displaced,
> where the cry of distress will be heard no more—not on the subway, not among our most vulnerable neighbors, and not—God, please—in Palestine and Israel,
> where lives will be cut short by violence no more,
> where weapons of displacement will be transformed into tools of inhabitation and placemaking,
> where dispossession and homelessness will be no more,
> where walls of exclusion and policies of deportation will be no more,
> where exploitation will be no more,
> where meaningless and demeaning labour will be no more,
> where children will be born for calamity no more,
> where ecological collapse and despoliation will be no more.[6]

No more, no more, no more. That is what I hear crying out in Meredith's life. The only way to inhabit a world of displacement is by embodying this vision of radical homecoming in community together, in solidarity, in joy and sorrow, and with the abiding and transforming presence of the Spirit of God in our midst. Maybe Meredith's story will help to show us the way. You see, sometimes hospitable homemaking happens in small acts of courage and love, of taking a stand and bearing witness . . . on the subway, at an encampment, in our neighborhood.

---

6. Isa 65:17–25.

6

Poverty, Justice, and the Fruit of the Spirit

In the beginning was fruitfulness.
    And in the end, there will be fruitfulness.
From the beginning to the end,
    it's always been about fruitfulness.

A fruitful creation.
A bringing-forth creation.

From the fruitfulness of the earth
    to the fruit-bearing trees,
        to the multiplying fruitfulness of birds, fish, and animals,
        to the fruitfulness of that creature who images the Creator,
it was all about fruitfulness.

In the beginning was fruitfulness.

And in the end there will be a tree of life,
> with fruit borne twelve months of the year,
> and with leaves that will be for the healing of the nations.

In the end there is fruitfulness.

From beginning to end, it has always been about fruitfulness.

Fruitfulness is what this story is all about.

> Be fruitful and multiply.

> I will make of you a great nation that will bear much fruit.

> Obey my word and you will be fruitful in all your ways.

> You shall share the fruit of your labors,
> and the poor will glean from your fields.

> Israel is a vineyard and the covenant God is the vinedresser.

> In exile you are to be fruitful and multiply.

> I will make the wilderness bloom and bear rich fruit.

> They shall plant vineyards and drink their wine,
> and they shall plant gardens and eat their fruit.

This is Israel's story,
> the story of fruitfulness in covenant,
> the story of a fruit-bearing creation,
> the story of a fruitful community of justice,

> and yet . . .

a story of fruitlessness when covenant is broken,
a story of bitter fruit when paths of idolatry are followed,
a story of injustice and oppression when fruitfulness is hoarded.

So, Jesus comes and tells stories of fruitfulness to remind the people.

There was this sower and he sowed his seed . . .

The kingdom of God is like the smallest seed . . .

A man planted a vineyard . . .

I am the vine, you are the branches . . .

You will know them by their fruit . . .

Fruitfulness,
    it's always been about fruitfulness,
    the truth of the gospel has always been in the fruit it bears.

And the fruit of the Spirit, Paul says,
    is love, joy, peace,
    patience, kindness, generosity,
    faithfulness, gentleness, and self-control.

Sounds good.
Sounds like a fulfillment of our deepest longings and hopes.
But the reality seldom meets the vision.

The fruit of the Spirit is love . . .
    while 25,000 die daily from starvation around the world
    and we live in a culture of deepening enmity.

The fruit of the Spirit is joy . . .
    while six million languish in refugee camps
    and there is an epidemic of depression in our land.

The fruit of the Spirit is peace . . .
>   while the nations continue to erupt into war
>   and we remain in deep conflict within ourselves and with others.

The fruit of the Spirit is patience . . .
>   while a billion people wait in vain for their daily bread,
>   and we demand immediate gratification.

The fruit of the Spirit is kindness . . .
>   while more than half of all Indigenous children in Canada live in poverty,
>   and sometimes we're just too overwhelmed to care.

The fruit of the Spirit is generosity . . .
>   while support for the poorest in our midst declines,
>   and we applaud tax cuts for the richest.

The fruit of the Spirit is faithfulness . . .
>   while treaties are broken and constitutions are desecrated,
>   and sexual fidelity has given way to consumptive acquisition.

The fruit of the Spirit is gentleness . . .
>   while white supremacy brutalizes migrants and people of color,
>   and politics devolves to the spectacle of professional wrestling.

The fruit of the Spirit is self-control . . .
>   while an addictive culture serves up an insatiable orgy of consumption,
>   and, well, we're all addicts.

You will know them by their fruit, Jesus says.

Paul brings this whole story of fruitfulness into sharp focus
>   when he writes about the fruit of the Spirit.

Of Prophets, Priests and Poets

That Spirit who hovered over the waters in the beginning,

that Spirit who led the children of Israel
    from the fruitlessness of the empire
    through the wastelands of the desert
    to a land rich in fruit,

that Spirit who breathed through the writing of the Scriptures,

that Spirit who would lead the exiles home from Babylon,

that Spirit who inspired the prophets with visions of fruitfulness,

that Spirit who rests upon the One
    who proclaims the Jubilee
    of renewed fruitfulness in Israel,

that Spirit who falls upon the disciples at Pentecost
    to lead the young church in paths of fruitfulness,

that Spirit, says Paul, bears rich fruit in our lives.

And that fruit is named:
    love
    joy
    peace
    patience
    kindness
    generosity
    faithfulness
    gentleness
    self-control

This is the fruit that the Spirit seeks to cultivate in us.
This is the fruit that has been at the heart of the story all along.

And just as Israel's story is one of fruitfulness and barrenness,
    a story of rich blessing and crushing curse,
    a story of faithfulness and infidelity,
so also is our own story deeply ambiguous.

We know the fruit of the Spirit when we see it,
    and we are painfully aware of how our own lives do not bear such fruit.

We long for the Spirit to bear rich fruit in our lives,
    we strive for such fruit,
    we even will submit ourselves to certain spiritual disciplines
    to cultivate such deeply spiritual virtues.

It is true—we are known by our fruit,
    and we embrace the way of the Spirit
    so that our very character will be shaped by the Spirit's fruit;
these will be the virtues that direct our paths so profoundly
    that such fruit will become second nature to us,
    become simply the most natural way in which we engage the world.

This is deeply personal stuff, friends,
    but we also need to remember
    that these virtues, this fruit of the Spirit,
    cannot be limited to personal morality.

You see, these are public virtues.

If the fruit of the Spirit is the fruit by which we will be known,
then this means nothing if our political, economic,
agricultural, ecological, cultural, and social lives
are not shaped by the likes of
    love
    joy
    peace

    patience
    kindness
    generosity
    faithfulness
    gentleness
    self-control

Here's the thing—
if we reduce the fruit of the Spirit
    to personal piety
    and private virtue,
then the fruit of the Spirit will be co-opted
    by the forces of oppression,
and we will become comfortable in a world
    of poverty and injustice,
and the Spirit will be grieved.

The fruit of the Spirit is love:
    a sacrificial love in a world of market exchange,
    a free gift in a world where everything has its price,
    a suffering love in which injustice never has the final word.

The fruit of the Spirit is joy:
    a deep joy in a world of manufactured desire,
    a contented joy in a world of insatiable consumption,
    a joy soaked in sorrow that will not be reduced to a cheap
        happiness.

The fruit of the Spirit is peace:
    an all-embracing shalom in a world bleeding from its wars,
    a peace rooted in justice in the face of the war on the poor,
    a covenant of peace in a creation groaning in travail.

The fruit of the Spirit is patience:
> a quiet, non-anxious patience because we know who saves this world,
> a patience juxtaposed to our culture of quick fixes and immediate gratification,
> a patience that is committed for the long haul.

The fruit of the Spirit is kindness:
> a deep disposition of care in a world of harshness and indifference,
> an empathy that weeps with those who weep,
> an openheartedness that refuses an aggressive egocentric lifestyle.

The fruit of the Spirit is generosity:
> an economics of enough in the face of unspeakable affluence,
> a generosity that shares the fruitfulness of creation with the most vulnerable,
> a generosity that makes poverty history, by making affluence history.

The fruit of the Spirit is faithfulness:
> a faithfulness to our God who is more concerned with obedience

than effectiveness and results,
> a faithfulness that will not break faith with our most impoverished brothers, sisters, and siblings,
> a faithfulness that refuses to be slaves of the empire

because we are subjects of the kingdom.

The fruit of the Spirit is self-control:
> a self-control that can say "no" to our own pleasures for the sake of justice,
> a self-control that can secede from an affluent consumerist society,
> a self-control that can break our addiction to "more."

This is the fruit of the Spirit,
> this is who we are, if we are filled with the Spirit,
> this is where this story of fruitfulness becomes manifest in
>> our lives.

And there is no law against such things, writes Paul.

There is no law against
> love
> joy
> peace
> patience
> kindness
> generosity
> faithfulness
> gentleness
> self-control

But if our lives are shaped by this fruit of the Spirit
> then we will face social disapproval,
we will face defensiveness in our churches,
> in our families and in our communities,
and we will find ourselves at odds with
> the principalities and powers that rule our world.

If we live by the Spirit,
> if the fruit of the Spirit is cultivated in our lives,
> then we will walk by the Spirit.

Refusing the idolatrous direction of the spirits of this age,
> we will submit our lives to the leading of the Spirit of God.

And this Spirit will lead us in paths of justice,
this Spirit will lead us to embody such fruit in everything we do,
this Spirit will make us into a community of
> love

joy
peace
patience
kindness
generosity
faithfulness
gentleness
self-control

May it be so.
Come, Holy Spirit, come.
Amen.

7

Faithfulness and Justice
Reformed Faith in the Face of Empire

I've always had the same problem with my Bibles.
From the very beginning of my Christian faith, some fifty-five years ago,
my Bibles have tended to fall apart.

My last Bible was an NRSV held together by duct tape.
> I couldn't read the first three chapters of Genesis in that one anymore,
> and Colossians was so marked up and worn that the pages were literally falling apart.

And before I started using the NRSV,
> my NIV also fell apart—its binding totally broken.

What is interesting to me is that where the first break happens
> in my old NIV is precisely at Psalm 33;
> a second break happens at Jeremiah 2,
> and then a third at Matthew 24.

Perhaps we could call the destruction of my Bibles over the years
> the result of an overly zealous practice
>> of the Reformation principle of *sola Scriptura*, Scripture alone.

I could only surmise why the second and third breaks
> in the binding of my NIV occurred where they did,
> but the break at Psalm 33 makes total sense to me.

You see, Psalm 33 is not only one of my favorite psalms,
> and not only includes one of my favorite verses in the Bible,
> it is also a psalm that encapsulates
> what I take to be the heart of a Reformed vision of life,
> the heart of Reformed theology,
> and the reason why I found myself drawn so early in my Christian walk
> to a Reformational worldview.

The debates about "justification by faith"
—whether in the sixteenth century or today—
are not what brought me to embrace a Reformed understanding of Christian faith.

Nor, I confess, did the so-called "five points of Calvinism,"
—reflecting a debate at the end of the seventeenth century—
lead me into the embrace of Reformed faith.

While these theological debates were important in their historical context,
they have always been too abstract for me.
They've never really touched me where I live.

A deeply Reformed worldview captured my imagination
in the context of a campus ministry community
at the University of Toronto in 1974.[1]

---

1. It was this campus ministry of the Christian Reformed Church that I was

In the face of so much world-denying piety,
>   here was a faith deeply rooted in the goodness of creation.

In the face of so much narrow biblicism
>   here was a faith that understood all of life
>   to be rooted in the creative Word of God.

In the face of a false sacred/secular dualism,
>   here was a faith that embraced God's rule over all of life.

In the face of a church that had become too comfortable and accommodated,
>   here was a faith that had the audacity to dethrone the powers
>   that be.

Here was a faith that animated my deepest longing
>   for whole-life discipleship.

A rich creational theology.
An understanding of all of life redeemed.
A comprehensive vision of the kingdom of God.
And a radical call to discipleship.

That's what I met in that Reformational campus ministry fellowship.
That's what I came to understand to be at the heart of the Reformation.

PSALM 33

And that's what we meet in Psalm 33.[2]

>   Rejoice in the Lord, O you righteous.
>   Praise befits the upright.
>   Praise the Lord with the lyre;

---

honored to serve from 1996 to 2020.
  2. NRSV, amended for inclusivity.

> make melody with the harp of ten strings.
> Sing to God a new song;
> > play skillfully on the strings, with loud shouts.
>
> For the word of the Lord is upright,
> > and all God's work is done in faithfulness.
>
> The Holy One loves righteousness and justice;
> > the earth is full of the steadfast love of the Lord.
>
> (33:1—5)

In this psalm we are invited into the heart of a covenantal imagination.

It's all there in the words that the psalmist loves to use:
> the *word* of God, the covenantal word of Torah,
> > meets a culture of deceit and political spin;
>
> the *faithfulness* of God, covenantal truthfulness,
> > meets a culture of infidelity and cover-up;
>
> the *righteousness* of God, God's call to holy integrity,
> > shines in the face of creation-and-soul-destroying sin and evil;
>
> the *justice* of God, the protection of the orphan, widow, and stranger,
> > stands before the injustice of a world of oppression.

No wonder the psalmist calls us to rejoice, praise, and sing!
Gratitude and praise befit those who follow such a God.

And then we come to my favorite verse.
It is here that my imagination was liberated.
It is here that we begin to plumb the depths of covenantal faith,
> the depths of the very nature of creation,
> > ... perhaps even the depths of God's very heart.

After singing that Yahweh "loves righteousness and justice,"
the psalmist proclaims that ...
> "the earth is full of the steadfast love of the Lord" (33:5).

Full of love.
Overflowing in love.
Dripping, saturated, soaked, running over in love.

And not just any love.
This is steadfast love.
This is covenantal love.
This is a faithful love.

As far as the psalmist is concerned,
love goes all the way down.

The *earth* is full of the Creator's love.
It is the very nature of the creation to be full of this love.

The earth, the soil, the micro-organisms,
the world and all that is in it,
is *full* of God's covenantal love,
permeated to its very core by steadfast love.

The Word that said, "let there be," is a Word of love.
The God who said, "this is good, good, good, good, very good,"
recognizes that goodness because the creation is wrought by divine love.

No wonder the psalmist exclaims:

> Let all the earth fear the Lord;
> let all the inhabitants of the world stand in awe of the Holy One.
> For the Creator spoke, and it came to be;
> commanded, and it stood firm (33:8–9).

Martin Luther King Jr. was undoubtedly right when he said that "the arc of the moral universe is long,
but it bends toward justice."

But why does it bend toward justice?
The universe bends toward justice
because it is rooted in love.

On crisp fall days it is easy to believe
that the earth is full of such steadfast love.

The delightful chill in the night air,
balanced by the warmth of the day;
the startling blue of the afternoon sky
and the breathtaking array of the night stars;
the stunning shock of color in the fall canopy
and the abundance of the harvest . . .
all bear witness to a creation of delight,
all testify to the steadfast love of the Creator.

That is . . . until you start to think about
the refugee crisis,
the rattling of the sabers of war,
the ecological desecration of our planet,
hundreds of missing Indigenous women and girls in Canada,
the machinations of the economics of greed,
the deceit of nations,
and the consumeristic emptiness of our culture.

Then it's a little difficult to see the world as full of such steadfast love.

So, what happens when the steadfast love of God meets the counsel of nations?
What happens when the word of the Lord meets the propaganda of empire?
What happens when the justice of God meets a world hell-bent on war?

Well . . . steadfast love turns to judgment:
    the counsel of nations is rendered null and void,

the propaganda is frustrated and unveiled as deceit,
the implements of war are rendered powerless.

That's why the psalmist continues:

> The Lord brings the counsel of the nations to nothing;
>   God frustrates the plans of the peoples.
> The counsel of the Lord stands for ever,
>   the thoughts of God's heart to all generations.
> Happy is the nation whose God is the Lord,
>   the people whom God has chosen as a heritage.
>
> The Lord looks down from heaven
> and sees all humankind.
> From where God sits enthroned the Lord watches
>   all the inhabitants of the earth—
> God fashions the hearts of them all,
>   and observes all their deeds.
>
> A king is not saved by his great army;
>   a warrior is not delivered by his great strength.
> The war horse is a vain hope for victory,
>   and by its great might it cannot save (33:10–17).

The corollary to a rich creation theology is a robust theology of history.
The God who calls creation into being is also the Lord of history.
The God who creates out of irrepressible love
> will not tolerate forever the arrogant forces of sin, greed, and hate.

And this God is not blind.
> The Lord sees what transpires in his world.
Nor is this God impotent.
> God moves in history to bring the mighty down from their thrones.

You see, the psalms do not call us to empty praise.
The psalms do not always fit well in the happy music

of the "worship set" at church.
The psalms do not present a sentimental world of sweet love.

No, the psalms envision a world that is full of the steadfast love of God,
> in the face of a culture hooked on avarice,
> in the face of a species who seem bound to betrayal,
> in the face of a culture taking a dive.

And that is why this psalm ends with hope.

> Truly the eye of the Lord is on those who fear God,
>> on those who hope in God's steadfast love,
> to deliver their soul from death,
>> and to keep them alive in famine.
>
> Our soul waits for the Lord;
>> our help and shield.
> Our heart is glad in the Lord,
>> because we trust in the holy name.
> Let your steadfast love, O Lord, be upon us,
>> even as we hope in you (33:18–22).

To sing this psalm is to hope in God's steadfast love,
> even when it doesn't seem like the earth is full of that steadfast love,
> even when it seems that the earth is wracked by hatred and violence.

To sing this psalm is to wait for the Lord,
> even against the evidence.

To sing this psalm is to pray longingly for that steadfast love
> to be manifest in our lives
> so that our hope will be fulfilled.

Psalm 33 invites us to live in a world of grace,
> a world that is full of the steadfast love of God,

with eyes wide open to all that would strip us of such love,
to all that would render the world so much less.

Every time I read this psalm,
I am reminded again and again
of the breadth and depth of a Reformed worldview
and why deep, deep gratitude is at the heart of John Calvin's theology.

I think that is why my old NIV fell open to this psalm so often
that the binding finally broke.

But what if it is more than just the binding that breaks?

What if it looks more and more as if the covenant itself is broken?

What if, over and over again, it is not the plans of the nations
    that are frustrated by God,
but it is the providence of God that is frustrated by the nations?

What if history looks as if a king *is saved* by his great army,
    the warrior *is victorious* by his own strength,
        and the war horse, along with other military procurements,
        are proven to be the only hope for victory?

What do you do when the earth is not filled with the steadfast love of God,
    but is drenched in blood,
    and filled with violence?

What do you do when history and hope won't rhyme?
When you have seen the future and it is murder?
When you have been waiting in hope for the Lord to be your help and shield,
    but you seem to have been left defenseless before the powers
        of this age,
    and it sure looks like you are waiting in vain?

FAITHFULNESS AND JUSTICE

What do you do when there is a tragic gap between vision and reality,
    an ever-widening gulf between worldview and world,
    a deep chasm between promise and fulfillment,
    a devastating conflict between theology and real life?[3]

Well . . . you keep singing.
But now you sing the blues.
Now you move from hymns of praise and rejoicing
    to painful, raw, honest, and abrasive songs of lament.

HABAKKUK

This brings us to the second chapter of Habakkuk.

Talk about living in the tragic gap.
Talk about a gulf between worldview and world.
Talk about a theological crisis of the deepest proportions.
This is Habakkuk's predicament.

Here is Habakkuk's devastating question:
what are we to do with Babylon?

How do we understand ourselves,
our place in history,
and our relationship with God,
in the light of the devastation
of Babylonian violence and exile?

Even if the Lord of history is to employ Babylon to execute judgment,
and even if such judgment is just by the terms of the covenant,
    how on earth . . .
—this earth full of the steadfast love of God! —
    how on earth can the God of steadfast love, justice, and
        righteousness

---

3. The phrase, "tragic gap," is from Palmer, "Broken-Open Heart."

be seen to be faithful to covenant promises
while allowing such unfettered violence to reign over God's people,
    and over creation?

This is Habakkuk's complaint.
This is the prophet's lament.

Almost echoing the psalmist's affirmation that,
    "Truly the eye of the Lord is on those who fear God" (Ps 33:18),
Habakkuk abrasively asks,
    "Why do you look on the treacherous,
    and are silent when the wicked swallow
    those more righteous than they?" (Hab 1:13b).

And so, the prophet says that he will stand at his watch post
    until he has an answer to his angry question.

And that is precisely where I have found myself many times over the years.
And that is where I met so many of the young adults
    who found a place in our campus ministry.

Standing at the watch post,
    crying out in lament,
    longing for the vision of Psalm 33 to be the reality of our lives,
    struggling to remain in this vision, to keep this faith,
        looking for hope across the horizon of our lives, with tears
            in our eyes,
    and refusing to put up with any quick and cheap answers.

What do we do with Babylon?
What do we do with Babylon's myths and guns,
    with Babylon's cultural power and economic control?
What do we do, as Martin Luther once put it,
    with the Babylonian captivity of the church?

This was Habakkuk's question.
This is the question that my students were asking with deepening intensity.
And this is the question that we must return to as a Reformation church.

Our crisis is one of vision.
While we want to see the world with Psalm 33 eyes,
our vision is cloudy at best and horrifying at worst.
In the face of Babylonian captivity, in the face of empire,
Habakkuk can't see with covenantal vision,
because the world in which he lives doesn't look much like the world of Psalm 33.

And so, God replies.

This is Habakkuk 2:2–17:

> Then the Lord answered me and said:
> Write the vision;
> > make it plain on tablets,
> > so that a runner may read it.
> For there is still a vision for the appointed time;
> > it speaks of the end, and does not lie.
> If it seems to tarry, wait for it;
> > it will surely come, it will not delay.
>
> Look at the proud!
> > Their spirit is not right in them,
> > but the righteous live by their faith.
> Moreover, wealth is treacherous;
> > the arrogant do not endure.
>
> They open their throats wide as Sheol;
> > like Death they never have enough.
> They gather all nations for themselves,
> > and collect all peoples as their own.

Shall not everyone taunt such people and,
with mocking riddles, say about them,

"Alas for you who heap up what is not your own!"
    How long will you load yourselves with goods taken
in pledge?
Will not your own creditors suddenly rise,
    and those who make you tremble wake up?
    Then you will be booty for them.

Because you have plundered many nations,
    all that survive of the peoples shall plunder you—
because of human bloodshed, and violence to the earth,
    to cities and all who live in them.

"Alas for you who get evil gain for your house,
    setting your nest on high
    to be safe from the reach of harm!"
You have devised shame for your house
    by cutting off many peoples;
    you have forfeited your life.

The very stones will cry out from the wall,
    and the plaster will respond from the woodwork.

"Alas for you who build a town by bloodshed,
    and found a city on iniquity!"
Is it not from the Lord of hosts
    that peoples labor only to feed the flames,
    and nations weary themselves for nothing?

But the earth will be filled
    with the knowledge of the glory of the Lord,
    as the waters cover the sea.

"Alas for you who make your neighbors drink,
    pouring out your wrath until they are drunk,
    in order to gaze on their nakedness!"
You will be sated with contempt instead of glory.
    Drink, you yourself, and stagger!

The cup in the Lord's right hand
> will come around to you,
> and shame will come upon your glory!

For the violence done to Lebanon will overwhelm you;
> the destruction of the animals will terrify you—
because of human bloodshed and violence to the earth,
> to cities and all who live in them.

There is still a vision, God tells Habakkuk,
> so make it plain that everyone can see.
There is still a vision in the midst of empire,
> and it is a vision of ending.
There is still a vision to end this horror.

It is a vision that lies just beyond the range of normal sight,
> you will have to strain your eyes a little,
> but once you see it, it will become as clear as day.

The tables will be turned on the empire,
> God assures the aggrieved prophet.

What goes around comes around.
The proud will fall from their elevated places.
The plunderer will be plundered.
The violence at the heart of your economy will revisit you.
And the terror of your rule will rebound upon you
> in a terrorism that will no know bounds.

Why?
> "... because of human bloodshed, and violence to the earth,
> to cities and all who live in them." (2:8b)

Twice, we hear God say these words in this short oracle:
> "... because of human bloodshed, and violence to the earth,
> to cities and all who live in them." (2:17b)

The insatiability of empire can never say "enough."
There is never enough wealth,
never enough power,
never enough imperial expansion,
never enough plunder.

Such insatiability is always covered in blood.

You see, bloodshed and violence beget bloodshed and violence—
that is an ironclad law of the universe.

Human bloodshed.
Violence to the earth.
Violence to the cities.
Violence to those who live in them.

The geopolitical violence of empire
    always, always, always
is manifest in ecological violence
and a violence at the heart of urban life.

Same old, same old.

But the God of shalom,
the God of justice,
the God of creation,
the God of love
    will have nothing of it.

And so the good news for Habakkuk
is that this whole idolatrous house of cards will fall.
And great will be its fall.

But there is more.

The empire and its violence cannot overturn God's love for creation.

And so, echoing the psalmist,
"the earth is full of the steadfast love of the Lord" (Ps 33:5),
    the oracle promises anew that,
"The earth will be filled
with the knowledge of the glory of the Lord,
as the waters cover the sea" (Hab 2:14).

Judgment is never the last word.
Judgment is always a word on the way,
a clearing of the way for a better word.

A world filled with violence,
overflowing in blood,
will be transformed.

This is the vision, Habakkuk.
Can you see it?

Maybe not.

Well then, if you are having a hard time seeing through the smoke,
    then just take a look at the proud.

Take a look at the masters in the empire.
Look at those who wield this destructive violence.
Look at the 1 percent who own more than 50 percent of all the world's wealth.
Take a good look.
What do you see?

Look at the billionaires.

They project such an ethos of ease and comfort.
They appear to be so secure and confident.
They appear to have everything under control,

descending their golden escalators,
riding in their golf carts,
strutting on the stage at their rallies.

But look more closely.
Do you see that their wealth is treacherous (2:6)?

Do you also see that such arrogance cannot endure?
Can you see that this is a world that can only implode?
Can you see that an economy of insatiable consumption,
    is like Death that has never had enough?
Can you see that such an economy will swell and bloat
    until it explodes?
Can you see that an imperial economy of exploitation and injustice
    will necessarily call forth rebellion?
Can you see that if you heap up what is not your own,
    if you set up a world economy of plunder,
    if you secure that economy through a geopolitics of bloodshed,
    and if you continue to do violence to the earth and to cities
    and to those who live in them,
then the whole thing is going to rebound on you?

Does it take too much just to open your eyes and see all of this?

And if you can't see it, then might you be able to hear it?

If you listen closely enough,
    can't you hear the cry of the stones in the walls
    and the plaster responding from the woodwork (2:11)?

We may be blind to what is going on,
    but the rest of creation is not.

We may simply see the shiny architecture of opulence
    in the construction boom all around us,
    but the building materials know better.

And so they, like all of creation, cry out in travail,
> call out in protest to how they are employed in service of idolatry,
> bear witness against a culture of treacherous wealth in the face of poverty,
> call out shameful development that builds grand homes for the rich,
> in the midst of a crippling crisis of housing affordability.

Shame, cry out the two-by-fours and the drywall. Shame!

But you and I, we've been through that, and this is not our fate.

Because you see, hidden in this vision,
> almost drowned out by this deconstruction of the empire,
> set in contrast to the proud in all of their disquiet,
there is another word.

St. Paul noticed it.
St. Paul knew that this was the heart of the matter.

St. Paul knew that while the empire was collapsing,
there was one anchor in the storm,
one thing that could be a foundation
for the reconstruction project of our culture, our economy, our lives.

> Look at the proud!
> Their spirit is not right in them,
> but the righteous live by faith. (Hab 2:4)

This was the answer to Habakkuk's lament.
The righteous live by faith.
Those who would seek justice live by faithfulness.
Faith and faithfulness are at the heart of the matter.

But there is a question here.
There is, not surprisingly, a matter of interpretation,
both in Habakkuk and when St. Paul cites Habakkuk in Romans.

Whose faith?

Both the NIV and NRSV offer one interpretation:
    "the righteous will live by *their* faith."

Now here is an interesting thing.
That interpretation of Habakkuk is well grounded in the Septuagint,
    that is, in the ancient Greek translation of the Hebrew text.
In fact, we could say that the Greek translation is itself an interpretation.

The Masoretic text, however (that is, the Hebrew text), is best translated:
    "The righteous will live by faithfulness."

Faithfulness.
Whose faithfulness?

ST. PAUL

It can go either way in Habakkuk,
and I think that St. Paul intentionally embraces both interpretations.
At the very beginning of his letter to the Romans—
a letter which will serve as the foundational text for the Reformation—
    Paul writes,

> For I am not ashamed of the gospel;
> it is the power of God for salvation to everyone who has faith,
> to the Jew first and also to the Greek.
> For in it the righteousness of God is revealed
> through faith for faith;

as it is written, "The one who is righteous will live by
faith." (Rom 1:16–17)

Through faith for faith.

Through the faithfulness of God
is born the faithfulness of God's people.
Our faith is a response called forth by God's faithfulness.

And Paul will go on to say that God's faithfulness,
    to a creation full of steadfast love,
    to a covenant with Abraham,
    to the vision of Psalm 33,
    and to the oracle of Habakkuk,
is manifest in one man—Jesus the Messiah.

That is why over and over again in the first seventeen verses of Romans,
    Paul refers to the gospel, the gospel, the gospel.

The gospel of God, rooted in the Torah, writings and prophets,
    is the good news of Jesus (1:1–2).

The gospel of God is that the promises are fulfilled in Jesus,
    through his resurrection from the dead (1:3).

The gospel of God proclaims Jesus as Lord,
    against all false challengers to the throne (1:4).

The gospel of God has gone throughout the world,
    and is being proclaimed at the very heart of the empire (1:8, 15).

The gospel of God is the power of God for salvation
    for everyone who embraces the faithfulness of Jesus Christ (1:16).

In the gospel "the justice of God is revealed through faith for faith; as it is written, "The one who is just will live by faith"[4] (1:17–18).

Now these three words
—gospel, faithfulness, and justice—
are at the symbolic heart of the Roman empire.

Just as Habakkuk is struggling with God's faithfulness
    in the face of the Babylonian empire,
so also is Paul addressing Christians living at the center of the Roman empire.

And you have to remember that when Paul reaches back to Habakkuk,
    he is not engaging in cheap prooftexting.
No, he reaches for that one line from Habakkuk 2 ("the righteous live by faith")
    within the whole context of Habakkuk's critique of empire.
That is why Habakkuk is so useful to Paul:
they are facing the same kind of imperial context.

And in the face of the empire's boast . . .

    that Roman "justice" was the apex of civilization;
    that the gods had bestowed "faithfulness" on Rome;
    that the only good news, the only "gospel" worth listening to came from Rome;
    that Caesar was the lord of all, and the one through whom salvation is secured . . .

Paul proclaims that there is only one Lord
    and his name is Jesus;
there is only one Savior,
    and he is the Messiah;

---

4. There are good reasons to translate the Greek word *dikaiosynē* as "justice," carrying with it the overtones of the two Hebrew words for justice (*mishpat*) and righteousness (*tsedaqah*). See Keesmaat and Walsh, *Romans Disarmed*, 11–12.

there is only one gospel that has real power
    and it blows away Rome's imperial propaganda;
there is only one God who is faithful;
and there is only one justice and it is the justice of this God.

REFORMATION

Calvin and Luther knew
that Paul's letter to the Romans was explosive.

And so, with this epistle ringing in their ears,
    they led a reformation of the church of Jesus Christ.
They attempted to embrace anew the power of the gospel,
    the depths of God's faithfulness,
    the expansive nature of the promises,
    and the radical call to discipleship.

The Reformation was rooted in an interpretation of Scripture
that addressed the social, religious, and political struggles of its time.

As the Reformers allowed Scripture to challenge tradition,
so also did they allow biblical faith to address all of life.

Luther and Calvin listened deeply to God's voice in Scripture
    to address the pressing questions of their time.

To be faithful to them we must do no less.

And so, in the face of the accommodation of the church to Nazism in the twentieth century, Reformed Christians wrote the Barmen Declaration as a clear
articulation of Reformed faith during the Third Reich.
Jesus, not the Führer, was Lord,
and the gospel, not fascist ideology, is the path of salvation.[5]

---

5. See https://www.ekd.de/en/The-Barmen-Declaration-303.htm.

And when the Reformed tradition was corrupted
by racist and colonial ideology,
those most deeply committed to a radically Reformed faith in South Africa
produced the Belhar Confession,
declaring apartheid to be the heresy that it is.
They called the church back to a unity that transcends racial boundaries,
a societal reconciliation befitting of the gospel,
and the justice that is at the heart of justification.[6]

And more recently,
when so much of the white evangelical church
has been taken captive by a new form of fascism
in the cult of Trumpism in the United States,
a Reformational impulse requires
a "reclaiming of Jesus" from this cultural distortion,[7]
and a clear stance against any form of Christian nationalism.[8]

If we are to name ourselves as Reformed,
if we are to honor the Reformation in the twenty-first century,
> then we will need to embrace anew this comprehensive vision,
> we will need to continue to read and interpret the Scriptures in all of their transformative power,
> and we will need to embrace a gospel that sets us free

---

6. See https://www.pcusa.org/site_media/media/uploads/theologyandworship/pdfs/the_belhar_confession-rogers.pdf.

7. A powerful video presentation of the "Reclaiming Jesus" statement can be found at https://sojo.net/media/reclaiming-jesus-time-crisis. The text can be accessed here: https://cac.org/daily-meditations/reclaiming-jesus-2018-06-19/.

8. See the "Christians Against Christian Nationalism Statement," at https://www.christiansagainstchristiannationalism.org/statement. Addressing similar concerns the Hungarian Evangelical Fellowship released a powerful and comprehensive statement against the distortion of Christian liberty in Hungary. Their Advent statement from 2019 can be accessed here: https://www.change.org/p/everybody-advent-statement-of-the-hungarian-evangelical-fellowship.

from our own Babylonian captivity.

Keep faith, dear friends, and you will see clearly.
Keep faith, embrace a righteous justice,
    and the vision will open up to you.
God is faithful.

The earth is indeed full of the Creator's steadfast love.
The gospel is the power of God for salvation to all.
For in this gospel, the justice of God is revealed
    through faithfulness for faithfulness.
As it is written: "the one who is just will live by faith."

8

On Not Forgetting Who You Are
A Targum

On the Sunday before the US election that saw Donald Trump reelected to the presidency, I wrote a targum specifically focused on Colossians 3:1–17, but with also a nod to the preceding passage (Colossians 2:8–23).[1] A targum is an expansive paraphrase on an ancient text that attempts to imagine what that text might sound like if it were written not two thousand years ago, but just the other week.[2] What happens if we take the extensive character ethic that Paul outlines in that amazing chapter, paying close attention to the imperial context in which he offered this vision of life, and reimagine this text as if it were written to us in our own socio-historical context? How might Paul have written that section of Colossians if he knew of the rise of white Christian nationalism, of Trumpism, of the divisions of our own time, indeed, of the church being taken captive by an ideology that is counter to the gospel? How might Colossians 3 speak a word of hope and

---

1. I encourage you to read these passages first, then read the targum, and then return to the passages again for a second reading.

2. On the genre of targum and the criteria by which a biblical targum can be evaluated, see Keesmaat and Walsh, *Romans Disarmed*, 34–36.

correction into our lives at this time in history? How might this character ethic help form us in our discipleship in the years to come? Perhaps it would look something like this . . .

ON NOT FORGETTING WHO YOU ARE

So friends . . .
you know the story.
You know where you are.

You know that there are forces of oppression all around you.
You know that they will try to take your imaginations captive.
You know that it is all rooted in deceit.
You know that the myth of exceptionalism, of "greatness," is a lie, regardless of who spouts it.
You know that a self-righteous ideology of exclusion is literally a dead end.
You know that puffed-up, narcissistic demagogues are fakes, they have no substance.
You know that the idolatry of wealth, nation, and power is at the heart of it all.

And . . . you know who you are.

You know that this story of empire is not your story,
and the national anthem is not your song.
You know that you have died to this culture of death.
You know Christ has disarmed these forces of empire on the cross.
You know that you have been buried with Christ in baptism.
You know that you have been raised with Christ to new life.
You know that in Christ, you are no longer subject to the demands of empire.
You know that in Christ you have a different story, a different song.

So then, why do you still play by the rules of the empire?
Why does that story continue to have a hold on you?

Of Prophets, Priests and Poets

Why is your imagination so constricted?
Why do you live pretty much like everyone else lives?

If you've been raised with Christ,
then let your imaginations be set free
by his loving rule, at the right hand of God.

It's not what goes on in Washington or Ottawa that matters.
It isn't Wall Street or Bay Street that rules this world.
That's not where the real sovereignty lies for you.

The risen One is the ascended One,
so let your minds and let your hearts
be directed by the One on the throne.

Set your minds on the sovereignty of the risen One,
and be set free from the earthly principalities and rulers
that have no imagination beyond the stock reports and GDP.

Jesus is Lord, not the market.

Secede from this culture of death
and live in the kingdom of life.

Seek first this kingdom, this rule of justice,
this restoration of all things,
because that is where your real identity lies.

You know who you are,
but you live in the tragic gap between
that knowledge of transformed identity,
and the present reality of brokenness, compromise, and failure.

Think of it as being hidden in Christ.
Jesus knows who you are.
And in Christ you know who you are.

But just as his full restoration of all things
has not yet been fully realized,
so also are we all in the process of full reconciliation,
the process of coming fully into ourselves in Christ.

But here's the deal.

When Christ is revealed,
when Jesus returns,
when the full redemption of creation is accomplished,
then we will also be revealed . . .
and it will be in glory.

The glory that is the presence of God,
fully at home with us in the new earth;
the glory that is the realization of our calling
as caretakers, gardeners, homemakers in that new earth . . .
that is where this story is going.

So don't get side tracked by a false heaven theology
of "glory land."
Don't sell out the rich vision of creation restored
for a cheap hope in an otherworldly glory in heaven.

God's glory is manifest here,
on this good earth for which Christ died.
And your glory is manifest here,
when your life is healed and restored,
when your life is filled with the presence of the Holy One.

You know who you are.

In Christ you have died.
In Christ you were buried.
In Christ you have been raised.
In the ascended Christ your imaginations have been set free.

In the return of Christ will you be fully redeemed to home in creation.

This is your story. This is your song.

Don't lose the plot.

Don't forget who you are.

SECEDING FROM THE BIG LIE

And . . . don't allow your lives to be subsumed again
in the deathly patterns of life, the deathly practices
of this idolatrous culture of death.

These powers of death are so overwhelming,
that we need to kill them before they kill us.

So put to death, my friends,
whatever blinds you to the path of life,
whatever will hold you captive to this culture of death.

You know what I'm talking about.
It's not all about sex,
but our insatiable sexual appetites,
our consumptive sexuality,
the violence of it all, the disrespect,
the lack of intimacy,
and the absence of deep fidelity,
is but an image of the consumerist idol that rules our lives.

That is a god of exploitation and anger.
That is a god of resentment and retribution.

And that is a god of greed,
of avarice, of endless growth.
That is the god of a cancer cell.

The whole edifice, the whole culture,
the whole ideology, the whole system,
is rooted in such greed,
constructed in the image of a false god.

And I tell you friends,
the Creator who called all of creation to being in love,
the Christ who reconciled all things on a cross,
will not abide such idolatry,
will not sit idly by as this creation of delight is desecrated,
will not be passive in the face of such disobedience to God's loving rule.

No, friends, out of God's incurable love,
and in the depth of God's grief before what has transpired,
God will respond in judgment.

You see, the world matters that much to God.
God cannot simply turn a blind eye to such injustice.

And from such injustice,
from such idolatry,
you have been set free.

The story of the empire is no longer your story.
The catchy pop song of consumerism is no longer your song.
Nor are the anthems of national superiority and exceptionalism.

So, telling a different story, and singing a different song,
do not allow the emotional dynamics of our conflicted culture
distort how you experience and talk about the world and our neighbors.

My goodness, the discourse of anger, wrath and malice
has dominated the public sphere, hasn't it.

Of Prophets, Priests and Poets

Once deceit replaces truth, it is no surprise that slander
is everyday talk these days.

Once you have bowed the knee to idols,
abusive speech becomes the lingua franca.

Once you have lost the vision of creation as a home of welcome
for God, for humanity, for all of creation,
then language of "deportation" and "poisoned blood,"
"the enemy within," and "drill baby drill,"
become a powerful discourse of violence in our time.

Once the imperial god of nationalism
has taken hold of a culture,
talk of taking possession of other countries
is simply a matter of the manifest destiny of an exceptional empire.

And it's all rooted in the lie.
The big lie.
About who God is,
about who we are,
and about the nature of the world.

It is all a lie.

A distortion of God as the guarantor of the nation state
and legitimation of the systems of the world.

A distortion of our fellow humans,
dismissed as garbage and vermin,
and not recognized as created in the image of God.

A distortion of the nature of the world,
reduced to resources for an economics of unceasing growth and extraction,
and not loved as creation, co-subjects of the covenant with the Creator.

In such a context, my friends,
in the face of such threats and temptations,
don't forget who you are.

Don't lose the plot of the story.

Don't start singing the songs of empire all over again.

A NEW SET OF CLOTHES

Remember, dear siblings,
you were buried in Christ . . . naked.
All the old clothes of empire were stripped off.
All the trappings of power,
the posturing of status,
the uniforms of nationalism,
the presumption of privilege . . .
it was all stripped off.

And you have clothed yourselves with a new self,
a new identity,
a new place of belonging,
renewed in knowledge,
redesigned for a new story,
reflective of a new plot line,
no longer bearing the image of idolatry,
but being renewed in nothing less than the image of God,
to which you have been called from the beginning.

Renewed in the image of the Creator,
not the emperor.

Renewed in the image of the Creator,
not the content creators.

Renewed in the image of the Creator,

not the image of any pop star, politician, or billionaire.

Renewed in the image of the Creator,
so get busy, dear friends,
bearing that image,
engaging in loving restoration,
constantly having your imaginations renewed,
and . . . recognizing your neighbor in that image.

And, as scandalous and as impossible as this might sound,
that is why, in this renewal there is no longer,

"American" and alien,
naturalized citizen and immigrant,

Jew or Palestinian,
Russian or Ukrainian,

male, female, or trans,
straight or queer,

rich and poor,
Black, white, Hispanic, or Asian,

laborer and manager,
slave and free,

because Christ is all and in all.

The walls of division,
the systems of exclusion and privilege,
the binaries that keep us in boxes,
the categories of in and out, us and them,
are all dismantled, disarmed, stripped of their power,
in this renewal of all things in Christ,
in this renewal of community in the image of the Creator.

And so, dear friends, don't forget who you are,
and live up to your identity in Christ.

It's time to put on some new clothes.
It's time to adorn ourselves,
to embody in our life together and in the world,
the clothing of those renewed in the image of God,
the clothing of those who are in Christ.

THE SHAPE OF THE RENEWED COMMUNITY

And you know where it all starts, don't you?
If we are called to image God,
then we begin with *compassion*.

Clothe yourselves in compassion.
In the face of a world of sorrow and hurt,
find yourselves where God would be found,
in the midst of the pain.

Where there is pain because of oppression,
where there is sorrow because of ecological degradation,
where there is hurt in the world,
that is where you should be.

Clothe yourselves with compassion,
be those who are in the midst of suffering.

Renewed in the image of God,
imagine this world through the tear-filled eyes of pain.

This isn't the prom that we are getting dressed for.
No, we are called to enter into the war zones of life.

So bear each other's pain,
as you embrace the pain of a broken world.

And when you are tempted with bitterness
wear the cloak of *kindness*.

If you are to sustain a life of compassion,
then you also need to be clothed in kindness.

This isn't a sentimental "be nice to everyone,"
but a more radical commitment to neighborliness.

Recognizing your neighbor as created in the image of God,
extend to your neighbor the care and generosity of kindness.

And recognize not only all people, but all of creation,
as your neighbors, as your kin.

What we're talking about is a kindness
that permeates "all my relations."

A kindness that is at the heart of our lives in our places,
at the heart of our homemaking in our habitats.

Such a life cannot be clothed in arrogance.

Self-serving arrogance only sees other people
and the rest of creation,
as either threat or opportunity for control.

No, my friends, these are not clothes of power that we are wearing,
but clothes of *humility*.

Engage the world, live lives of humility,
without swagger or self-important superiority.

When you are too sure of yourself,
wear humility as you listen, ever so closely,
to the voice of creation, the voice of your neighbor, the voice of God.

I guess what I'm talking about here is akin to *meekness* or *gentleness*.

In a world that is all about mastery,
all about control,
all about being better than those "other" people,
all about a sense of ownership and proprietary rights,
we are to clothe ourselves in a meekness
that receives the world as a precious gift;
we need to embody a gentleness
that will lovingly attend to the bruised, the vulnerable.

Lord knows we have enough bullying, enough manipulation,
enough power grabs in our lives,
in our politics,
in our neighborhoods,
in our churches,
in our workplaces.

Let us be wearing different clothes, friends.
Let our lives bear witness to a gentleness that is
strong in humility, kindness, and compassion.

But don't expect quick results.
There is no quick fix to our struggles,
There is no easy solution to life distorted by idolatry.

These are not clothes for a short walk in the park,
but for the long and dangerous journey through the ruins
of our culture on the way to the coming rule of Christ.

So, be *patient.*

Both with yourselves and with each other.
Indeed, be patient with God.
God, after all, has been patient with us.

Of Prophets, Priests and Poets

We are, as one of your prophets has written,
both "working and waiting" for the miracle of new creation.[3]

We are working,
and that is why we are putting on our work clothes.

But we are also waiting.
It will take "a lot of doing to see this undoing through"
(as another one of your prophets has noted),[4]
and ultimately, we don't bring that renewal,
we don't, in the end, achieve that miracle.

So we will need to be clothed with patience on this path.

And, you know, we may be putting on new clothes,
but the old clothes still fit,
the old practices still have a hold on us,
the old self doesn't die easily,
and neither does the metanarrative of empire.

So, here's the sad truth, beloved community,
here's the hard thing, friends in Christ,
we will not always live with *compassion, kindness,
humility, meekness,* and *patience.*

Too often, these will not be the clothes that you will wear.

Cold heartedness, self-serving anger,
arrogance, harshness and impatience,
will too often be the reality of our lives together.

And that is why we must also
wear the robes of *forgiveness* in our lives.

---

3. Bruce Cockburn, "Waiting for a Miracle," *Waiting for a Miracle,* 1987.
4. Ani DiFranco, "To the Teeth," *To the Teeth,* 1999.

Forgiveness, not retribution.
Forgiveness, not vengeance.

You see, retribution and vengeance
is the wardrobe of empire,
not the clothing of Christ.

So, my friends, where there is disappointment and hurt,
where there is grievance and injury,
allow a spirit of forgiveness to restore what is broken,
and to lead you on the path of reconciliation.

May you wear *compassion, kindness,*
humility, meekness, patience, and *forgiveness,*
as the very clothes of your lives.

But above all,
clothe yourselves with *love,*
which binds everything together in perfect harmony.

Have you been keeping count?

Six virtues, beginning, of course, in compassion,
that then take us to kindness, humility, meekness,
patience, and forgiveness.

And all of this is good, very good.

But the seventh virtue,
the seventh manifestation of what it means to be in Christ,
the seventh way that the story of Jesus is embodied in our lives,
is, of course, love.

The love that called creation into being,
the love that holds creation all together,
the love that is the heart of the covenant,

the love that was made flesh in Jesus,
the love that went to a Roman cross,
the love that constitutes the body of Christ,
is the love that "binds everything together in perfect harmony."

In a world of enmity,
in a world of violence,
in a world of oppression,
in a world of misplaced loves of nation, power and wealth . . .

we must be known by our love,
we must embody love in our politics,
love in our shopping practices,
love in community development,
love in housing,
love in the arts,
love in caring for our places in the world,
love for those most vulnerable,
love for those most despised.

And if such love is manifest in our lives,
then the *peace* of Christ
will so rule in our hearts
that we will be a witness for peace,
advocates for peace,
agents of shalom,
on the streets,
in the halls of power,
in our households,
in our vocations,
in our communities.

We will seek the peace of the nations . . .

the peace, the shalom, the flourishing

of Indigenous neighbors longing for clean water, real control over their lives,
and healing from generations of genocide;

the peace, the shalom, the flourishing
of Palestinians removed from their land and subject to genocidal violence,

the peace, the shalom, the flourishing
of all people who are subjected to violence and conflict around the world;

the peace, the shalom, the flourishing
of migrants vilified and scapegoated by an angry population;

the peace, the shalom, the flourishing
of a land caught in ecological, economic, social, and political turmoil.

Moreover, friends, in a world of entitlement
and dissatisfaction,
in a world so absent of the peace and love
that we are talking about,
practice radical *gratitude*.

I know, it sounds counterintuitive.
There is so much to complain about.
There is so much to lament.
There is so much sorrow.

But compassion and gratitude need each other.
Compassion without gratitude gets lost in the pain.
Gratitude without compassion is cheap and self-congratulatory happiness.

No, friends, this is a story that goes deeper than all of that.
This is a story that begins in joy, begins in delight, begins in gratitude.

And so, dear siblings in Christ,
let gratitude permeate your lives;
let thankfulness set you free from bitterness,
and empower you for the hard work of restoration.

Remember, we are talking here
about being revealed with Christ "in glory."

This is a vision of creation-wide restoration and homecoming.

So, as you make a home together,
as you dwell together in covenantal love,
let the *word of Christ dwell* in you richly;
let this living and transforming word
be at home in your lives together,
so that you will be blessed with wisdom.

That's why I've been writing to you.

That's why we have struggled together,
in thought, and in prayer,
throughout these days of trial.

It has all been so that we might grow in knowledge,
wisdom, and understanding,
so that we might bear the fruit of the gospel in all of life.

And Lord knows, we need more music.

You see, this knowledge, this renewal of our identities in Christ,
this restoration of the image of God among us,
needs to be sung.

Sung in the tears of compassion and of gratitude.
Sung with the blues and jazz, with cantatas and anthems,
and rock and roll.

So don't forget to sing.

Sing songs of joy and gratitude,
sing songs of lament and hurt,
sing odes to joy and odes to pain,
but sing.

Put on these clothes, dear community,
array yourself with these virtues,
so that whatever you do in word or deed,
whether it be
caring for your neighbors through the food bank
or engaging your employment as a site of service;
making love or building homes;
exercising hospitality or restoring the local watershed;
engaging the political process or making investment decisions . . .

whatever you do in word or deed,
indeed, the very fabric of your lives,
will be done in the name of Jesus,
and in deep, deep gratitude to God the loving Creator.

Put on the clothing of Christ, dear friends.
In the days ahead, our lives will depend on it.

Bibliography

Berger, Peter. *The Sacred Canopy*. Garden City, NY: Doubleday, 1967.
Bernstein, Richard. *The New Constellation: The Ethical-Political Horizons of Modernity/Postmodernity*. Cambridge: MIT Press, 1992.
Berry, Wendell. *Another Turn of the Crank*. Washington, DC: Counterpoint, 1995.
———. *The Gift of Good Land*. New York: North Point, 1981.
———. *Home Economics*. New York: North Point, 1987.
———. *The Selected Poems of Wendell Berry*. Washington, DC: Counterpoint, 1998.
———. *Sex, Economy, Freedom and Community*. New York: Pantheon, 1992.
———. *The Unsettling of America: Culture and Agriculture*. San Francisco: Sierra Club, 1986.
———. *What are People For?* New York: North Point, 1990.
Billings, J. Todd. "The Problem with TULIP, or more than TULIPS in this Field." *Reformed Journal*, March 1, 2011. https://reformedjournal.com/the-problem-with-tulip-or-more-than-tulips-in-this-field.
Boyle, Nicholas. *Who Are We Now? Christian Humanism and the Global Market from Hegel to Heaney*. Edinburgh: T&T Clark, 1998.
Bouma-Prediger, Steven. *Creation Care Discipleship: Why Earthkeeping is an Essential Christian Practice*. Grand Rapids: Baker Academic, 2023.
———. *Earthkeeping and Character: Exploring a Christian Ecological Virtue Ethic*. Grand Rapids: Baker Academic, 2020.
———. *For the Beauty of the Earth: A Christian Vision of Creation Care*. Grand Rapids: Baker Academic, 2001.
———. "Yearning for Home: The Christian Doctrine of Creation in a Postmodern Age." In *Postmodern Philosophy and Christian Thought*, edited by Merold Westphal, 169–201. Bloomington: University of Indiana Press, 1999.

BIBLIOGRAPHY

Bouma-Prediger, Steven, and Brian J. Walsh. *Beyond Homelessness: Christian Faith in a Culture of Displacement.* 15th Anniversary Edition. Grand Rapids: Eerdmans, 2023.

———. "Education for Homelessness or Homecoming: The Christian College in a Postmodern Culture." *Christian Scholar's Review* 32.3 (Spring 2003) 281–95.

———. "Response: If It Ain't Broke, Don't Fix it: A Response to Robin Klay and John Lunn." *Christian Scholars Review* 33.4 (Summer 2004) 443–50.

Bratt, James D., ed. *Abraham Kuyper: A Centennial Reader.* Grand Rapids: Eerdmans, 1998.

Brown, Malcom, and Graham Tomlin, eds. *Coming Home: A Theology of Housing.* London: Church House, 2020.

Brueggemann, Walter. *Hopeful Imagination: Prophetic Voices in Exile.* Philadelphia: Fortress, 1986.

———. *Interpretation and Obedience.* Minneapolis: Fortress, 1999.

———. *The Land: Place as Gift, Promise and Challenge in Biblical Faith.* 2nd ed. Minneapolis: Fortress, 2002.

———. *The Message of the Psalms: A Theological Commentary.* Minneapolis: Augsburg, 1984.

———. *The Prophetic Imagination.* Philadelphia: Fortress, 1978.

———. *Reality, Grief, Hope: Three Urgent Prophetic Tasks.* Grand Rapids: Eerdmans, 2014.

Coupland, Douglas. *Life After God.* New York: Pocket, 1995.

Daly, Herman, and John B. Cobb Jr. *For the Common Good.* Boston: Beacon Press, 1989.

Douglas, Mary. *Purity and Danger.* London: Routledge, and Kegan Paul, 1966.

Dykstra, Craig. *Vision and Character: A Christian Educator's Alternative to Kohlberg.* Eugene, OR: Wipf and Stock, 2008.

Fernhout, Harry. "Christian Schooling: Telling a Worldview Story." In *The Crumbling Walls of Certainty: Towards a Christian Critique of Postmodernity and Education,* edited by Ian Lambert and Suzanne Mitchell, 75–98. Sydney: Centre for the Study of Australian Christianity, 1997.

Geertz, Clifford. *The Interpretation of Cultures.* New York: Basic Books, 1973.

Goudzwaard, Bob. *Capitalism and Progress: A Diagnosis of Western Society.* Translated by Josina Van Nuis Zylstra. Toronto and Grand Rapids: Wedge and Eerdmans, 1979.

Groome, Thomas. *Sharing Faith: A Comprehensive Approach to Religious Education and Pastoral Ministry.* Eugene, OR: Wipf and Stock, 1991.

Hardin, Garrett. *Filters Against Folly.* New York: Penguin, 1985.

Hauerwas, Stanley. "The Christian Difference: Or Surviving Postmodernism." In *Anabaptists and Postmodernity,* edited by Susan and Gerald Biesecker-Mast, 144–61. Telford, PA: Pandora, 2000.

———. *A Community of Character.* Notre Dame: University of Notre Dame Press, 1981.

BIBLIOGRAPHY

Hauerwas, Stanley, and William Willimon. *Resident Aliens: Life in the Christian Colony.* Nashville: Abingdon, 1989.

Haught, John F. "Religious and Cosmic Homelessness: Some Environmental Implications." In *Liberating Life: Contemporary Approaches to Ecological Theology*, edited by Charles Birch, William Eakin and Jay B. McDaniel, 159–81. Maryknoll, NY: Orbis, 1991.

Hobson, Peter, and Louise Welbourne. "A Conceptual Basis for Transformative Christian Religious Education." *Journal of Christian Education* 40.1 (April 1997) 37–46.

Illich, Ivan. "Dwelling." *Co-evolution Quarterly* 41 (Spring 1984) 22–27.

Jackson, Wes. *Becoming Native to this Place.* Washington, DC: Counterpoint, 1996.

Keesmaat, Sylvia. *Paul and His Story: (Re)Interpreting the Exodus Tradition.* Sheffield: Sheffield Academic Press, 1999.

Keesmaat, Sylvia C., and Brian J. Walsh. *Romans Disarmed: Resisting Empire, Demanding Justice.* Grand Rapids: Brazos, 2019.

Klay, Robin, and John Lunn. "Reflection: Linking Education to Upward Mobility and Weaker Environmental Stewardship? A Response by Economists." *Christian Scholars Review* 33.4 (Summer 2004) 433–442.

Kohak, Erazim. "Of Dwelling and Wayfaring: A Quest for Metaphors." In *The Longing for Home*, edited by Leroy S. Rouner, 30–46. Boston University Studies in Philosophy and Religion, volume 17. Notre Dame: University of Notre Dame Press, 1996.

Kozol, Jonathan. *The Night is Dark and I am Far From Home.* Boston: Houghton Mifflin, 1975.

Kunstler, James. *Geography of Nowhere: The Rise and Decline of America's Manmade Landscape.* New York: Simon and Schuster, 1993.

———. *Home from Nowhere: Remaking our Everyday World for the 21st Century.* New York: Simon Schuster, 1993.

Leach, William. *Country of Exiles: Destruction of Place in American Life.* New York: Pantheon, 1999.

Leopold, Aldo. *Sand County Almanac.* New York: Ballantine, 1970.

Levinas, Emmanuel. *Totality and Infinity: An Essay on Exteriority.* Translated by A. Lingis. Pittsburgh: Duquense University Press, 1969.

Lewis, C. S. *The Magician's Nephew.* New York: Macmillan, 1978.

Lundin, Roger. *The Culture of Interpretation: Christian Faith and the Postmodern World.* Grand Rapids: Eerdmans, 1994.

Middleton, J. Richard, and Brian J. Walsh. *Truth is Stranger Than It Used to be: Biblical Faith in a Postmodern Age.* Downers Grove, IL: InterVarsity, 1995.

Mouw, Richard. "Assessing Christian Scholarship: Where We've Been and Where We're Going," An address at the conference, "Christian Scholarship . . . For What?," Calvin College, September 2001. https://digitalcommons.calvin.edu/mouw_recordings/18/.

Nash, Ronald. *Worldviews in Conflict.* Grand Rapids: Zondervan, 1992.

Olthuis, James H. "On Worldviews." *Christian Scholars Review* 14.2 (1985) 153–64.

Orr, David. *Earth in Mind: On Education, Environment and the Human Prospect.* Washington, DC: Island, 1994.

———. *Ecological Literacy.* Albany, NY: SUNY Press, 1992.

Osborn, Bud. *Hundred Block Rock.* Vancouver: Arsenal Pulp, 1999.

———. *Keys to Kingdoms.* Vancouver: Get to the Point, 1999.

O'Sullivan, Edmund. *Transformative Learning: Educational Vision for the 21st Century.* Toronto: University of Toronto Press, 1999.

Palmer, Parker. "The Broken-Open Heart: Living with Faith and Hope in the Tragic Gap." *Weavings* 24.2 (March/April 2009) 1–12.

———. *To Know as We are Known: A Spirituality of Education.* San Francisco: Harper and Row, 1983.

Pohl, Christine D. *Making Room: Recovering Hospitality as a Christian Tradition.* Grand Rapids: Eerdmans, 1999.

Postman, Neil. *The End of Education: Redefining the Value of School.* New York: Vintage, 1996.

Rolston, Holmes III. *Environmental Ethics: Duties to and Values in the Natural World.* Philadelphia: Temple University Press, 1988.

Said, Edward. "Reflections on Exile." In *Out There: Marginalization and Contemporary Cultures*, edited by R. Ferguson, M. Gever, Trinh T. Minh-ha, and Cornel West, 357–66. New York: New Museum of Contemporary Art. Cambridge: MIT Press, 1990.

Schumacher, E. F. *Small is Beautiful.* New York: Harper and Row, 1973.

Smith, David I. *Learning from the Stranger: Christian Faith and Cultural Diversity.* Grand Rapids: Eerdmans, 2009.

Smith, David I., and Barbara Carvill. *The Gift of the Stranger: Faith, Hospitality, and Foreign Language Learning.* Grand Rapids: Eerdmans, 2000.

Smith, James K. A. *Awaiting the King: Reformed Public Theology.* Grand Rapids: Baker Academic. 2017.

———. *Desiring the Kingdom: Worship, Worldview and Cultural Formation.* Grand Rapids: Baker Academic, 2009.

———. *Imagining the Kingdom: How Worship Works.* Grand Rapids: Baker Academic, 2013.

Stronks, Gloria, and Doug Blomberg, eds. *A Vision With A Task: Christian Schooling for Responsive Discipleship.* Grand Rapids: Baker, 1993.

Taylor, Mark C. *Erring: A Postmodern A/Theology.* Chicago: University of Chicago Press, 1984.

Volf, Miroslav, and Ryan McAnnally-Linz. *The Home of God: A Brief Story of Everything.* Grand Rapids: Brazos, 2022.

Wachtel, Paul. *The Poverty of Affluence: A Psychological Portrait of the American Way of Life.* Philadelphia: New Society, 1989.

Walsh, Brian J. "Homemaking in Exile: Homelessness, Postmodernity and Theological Reflection." In *Renewing the Mind in Learning*, edited by

Doug Blomberg and Ian Lambert, 1–21. Sydney: Centre for the Study of Australian Christianity, 1998.
———. *Kicking at the Darkness: Bruce Cockburn and the Christian Imagination*. Grand Rapids: Brazos, 2011.
———. *Rags of Light: Leonard Cohen and the Landscape of Biblical Imagination*. Eugene, OR: Cascade, 2024.
———. "Sacred Space, Desecration and Reconciliation: A Story and Some Theses." *The Other Journal* 33. https://theotherjournal.com/2022/03/sacred-space-theses/.
———. *Subversive Christianity: Imaging God in a Dangerous Time*. 2nd ed. Eugene, OR: Cascade, 2014.
———. "Wake up Dead Man: Singing the Psalms of Lament." In *Get Up off Your Knees: Preaching the U2 Catalog*, edited by Raewynne J. Whitely and Beth Maynard, 37–42. Cambridge, MA: Cowley, 2003.
———. "Walk On: Biblical Hope and U2." In *Get Up off Your Knees: Preaching the U2 Catalog*, edited by Raewynne J. Whitely and Beth Maynard, 75–82. Cambridge, MA: Cowley, 2003.
Walsh, Brian J., and Sylvia C. Keesmaat. *Colossians Remixed: Subverting the Empire*. Downers Grove, IL: InterVarsity, 2004.
Walsh, Brian J., and J. Richard Middleton. *The Transforming Vision: Shaping a Christian World View*. Downers Grove, IL: InterVarsity, 1984.
Walsh, Brian J., and the Wine Before Breakfast Community. *Habakkuk Before Breakfast: Liturgy, Lament and Hope*. Eugene, OR: Cascade, 2020.
———. *St. John Before Breakfast*. Toronto: Books Before Breakfast, 2014.
Weisel, Eli. "Longing for Home." In *The Longing for Home*, edited by Leroy S. Rouner, 17–29. Boston University Studies in Philosophy and Religion, volume 17. Notre Dame: University of Notre Dame Press, 1996.
Wolterstorff, Nicholas. *Educating for Responsible Action*. Grand Rapids: Eerdmans, 1980.
Wright, Andrew. "Transformative Christian Education: New Covenant, New Creation. An Essay in Constructive Theology." *Journal of Education and Christian Belief* 2.2 (Autumn 1998) 93–108.
Wright, N. T. *History and Eschatology: Jesus and the Promise of Natural Theology*. Waco, TX: Baylor University Press, 2019.
———. *Jesus and the Victory of God*. London: SPCK 1996.
———. *The New Testament and the People of God*. Minneapolis: Fortress, 1992.
Wirzba, Norman. *From Nature to Creation: A Christian Vision for Understanding and Loving Our World*. Grand Rapids: Baker Academic, 2015.

www.ingramcontent.com/pod-product-compliance
Lightning Source LLC
Chambersburg PA
CBHW022123160426
43197CB00009B/1133